# WHY
# NEW ORLEANS
# MATTERS

# WHY NEW ORLEANS MATTERS

## TOM PIAZZA

ReganBooks
*An Imprint of* HarperCollins*Publishers*

HarperCollins books may be purchased for educational, business, or sales
promotional use. For information please write: Special Markets Department,
HarperCollins Publishers Inc., 10 East 53rd Street, New York, NY 10022.

FIRST EDITION

*Designed by Kris Tobiassen*

Printed on acid-free paper
Library of Congress Cataloging-in-Publication Data has been applied for.

ISBN 13: 978-0-06-112483-9
ISBN 10: 0-06-112483-4

05   06   07   08   09   RRD   10   9   8   7   6   5   4   3   2   1

FOR MARY, WHO WENT THROUGH IT TOO.

AND FOR EVERYONE WHO
LOVES NEW ORLEANS.

# WHY
# NEW ORLEANS
# MATTERS

# INTRODUCTION

On August 29, 2005, I sat in a kitchen in Malden, Missouri, watching televised images of my adopted hometown, New Orleans, sliding into chaos. Like tens of thousands of others who had evacuated the city, I breathed an initial sigh of relief when I saw that New Orleans had been spared the full effect of the long-predicted Category 4 hurricane named Katrina that had destroyed the Mississippi Gulf Coast towns of Biloxi, Gulfport, Waveland, Pass Christian, and Bay St. Louis, only to watch in horror and disbelief as cracks opened in two levees holding back the waters of Lake Pontchartrain and New Orleans began to fill with water.

Anyone who was alive and conscious that week will remember the images. First the Lower Ninth Ward, home to some of the poorest people in the area to begin with, St.

Bernard Parish, and New Orleans East filled, in places, to
the rooftops. People who had not been able to follow, or
believe, or even hear, the evacuation orders were trapped in
their houses, forced to climb to the second floors and often
to their attics, and finally to break through their own roofs,
sometimes with nothing more than a pocket knife, where
they waved desperately for someone to rescue them. Others waited on the sidewalk, luggage packed, for the buses
they thought were coming to take them to safety, eventually giving up and returning to their houses, where they
were trapped by the rising water.

Many who had not been able to evacuate the city
were told to go to the Superdome for shelter. Midway
through that Monday, August 29, the roof of the Superdome began to blow off. Toilets overflowed, there was no
organization, thin medical services, no real forethought,
and over the next day and a half the population at the
dome swelled from 10,000 to 20,000, to 25,000, to 30,000,
and higher. A man committed suicide by jumping from
one of the balconies, a harbinger of worse, much worse,
to come. People were kept inside by guards—at first to
keep them from going out into the storm and being killed
and later to keep them from illegally foraging for food or

fresh water. And, perhaps, to keep them from the television cameras as well.

Electricity had failed in the city, and soon the hospitals' generators ran out of power. Rising flood waters made rescue dangerous and sometimes impossible. Except for some walkie-talkies, all communications failed—home phones, police phones, cell phones. Looting began to break out, and then heavier looting—according to eyewitness accounts some police officers took part in the looting themselves—and by Wednesday gangs of armed thugs roamed the city at will, unchallenged, breaking into hospitals to steal medicine, robbing people on the street, and even shooting at rescue workers who were trying to save people from the roofs of their houses. One man, who had taken refuge in the D-Day Museum, reportedly saw a woman get gang raped on the sidewalk outside the museum's huge windows, powerless to stop it. At the Superdome, and then at the Morial Convention Center, the situation worsened. At the Superdome the preparations were inadequate and quickly overwhelmed; at the Convention Center, they were nonexistent. Corpses of neighbors, friends, family members, black and white, were scattered on the sidewalks; people had no sanitary facilities, no medical care, and the weakest were easy pickings for the predators among them. Thousands lived through scenes out of Goya or Hieronymus Bosch. Nobody came through to tell them at least what was happening, and why, and to give them some hope.

And yet they were luckier than their own neighbors and family members who could not get out of their attics in the flooded Ninth Ward, and whose cries could be heard throughout the week by rescue workers and reporters in shallow-bottomed boats, cruising the waters in shock and disbelief, heroically trying to save as many as they could. They saved many hundreds of lives, and they are the biggest heroes of that nightmare week, but there were many hundreds more to save, and the rescuers were an ad hoc, rag-tag group—blue-collar guys from Kenner, Cajun fishermen from southwestern Louisiana, whoever had the means and desire to help. Sheriff Harry Lee of neighboring Jefferson Parish seemed like the only person in Louisiana with an ounce of sense on that Monday when he issued an order to everyone in the parish who owned a shallow-draft boat to meet him in the parking lot of a shopping center and go out with him to save some people.

Others in New Orleans itself took matters into their own hands when they saw that no one else was going to help them. On Fox News, Greta Van Susteren interviewed a young African American man who looked to be in his teens; he had stolen a yellow school bus, loaded it with eighty people black and white, young and old, and drove them to Houston, depositing them at an already-full Astrodome. They were refused admittance at first, but when the Red Cross heard the story, they let them in. And then there were the stories and fragmentary television footage from the hospitals—doctors and nurses trying desperately to help patients by flashlight in un-air-conditioned crowded hallways and rooms, working intravenous machines and ventilators by hand in the impossible heat and stench. . . . By the time you read this book you will have seen plenty of such accounts. The situation, over the course of the week, went from frightening, to desperate, to indescribably brutal and sad, and finally to incomprehensible.

Like the rest of the country, and the world, I watched in anger, confusion, and disbelief. This was happening in the United States of America. Where was the plan? For years we had been told that such a storm making a direct hit on New Orleans was not just possible but also inevitable. For years we had been told that the failure of the levee system was inevitable. For years the government had been aware of a working model of just how the flooding would come. Now that it had happened, whatever plans had been made were obviously completely inadequate. To add insult to injury, the president of the United States, known for preferring faith to hard information, claimed on television that nobody could have foreseen the breaks in the levees.

The difference between cluelessness and mendacity became invisible in elected officials at every level of government as they scrambled to save face. As the week dragged on and the city sank into anarchy, one kept wondering where the National Guard was, where the Marines were, where the paratroopers were. Finally, on Friday, September 2, a full five days after the storm hit, some National Guard troops, fewer than two thousand, entered the city, driving in convoy through bumper-deep water, and arrived at the Convention Center—a place that no one will ever be able to look at again without a feeling of shame—where the corpses rotted on the sidewalks and young girls were raped in the labyrinthine halls and nooks. They distributed bottles of water to the first comers, and a hot meal, until the provisions ran out. Then, over that weekend, the city slowly began to receive the military and logistical help that it had needed since the previous Monday.

New Orleans was sustaining wounds that went far

beyond the merely physical and temporal. The city and its people were sustaining psychic and spiritual wounds from which recovery is not so straightforward.

Over the following week, there were the evacuees, the displaced citizens, a diaspora of historic proportions, many of whom had rarely if ever set foot outside their neighborhoods, much less their city. They went in buses to Houston, to Dallas, to Arkansas, and Missouri and Iowa; some went to Colorado, and to Minnesota and Utah. It would be impossible to overstate the degree of psychic and cultural dislocation involved. As with many traumas, it is like looking at the world through a warped window. Some things get slightly larger, some things slightly smaller. Straight lines appear to be slightly curved, or wobbly. There is constant psychic disjunction, as there was so memorably on the achingly beautiful fall morning of September 11, 2001—the eeriness of the beautiful day in front of you, the people in the community where you have found yourself, going about their lives in continuity with the past, set against your own discontinuity, your own images of the devastation of the city that is home for you. At its most intense it is like being in a centrifuge; the different parts of what is usually an integrated personality, mixed together under ordinary circumstances as if in solution, separate out into strata of different densities. At any given moment one is an exaggerated, or concentrated, version of some part of oneself—more generous, more selfish, more sensitive, more energetic, more lethargic, more violent, more passive, more insightful, more oblivious.

I felt all these things, and I was in a place with heat, water, medicine, food, air-conditioning at the push of a button, people to help out, people to care, television to give me up-to-date news, friends and family bombarding me with calls and e-mails. What about the man I saw on television, walking down the street holding two young boys, his sons, by the hands, wearing only a ragged T-shirt, crying in front of the news cameras, a man like many I had spent time around, a grown man, my age, reduced to tears in front of his sons and the eyes of the world because the rickety supports that he had managed to put together for himself and his family had blown away like dust in the breeze? Or the woman in labor who swam for thirty minutes through the sewage- and chemical-filled water, having contractions, searching for dry land where she could have her baby, after leaving her nine-year-old son to fend for himself?

These images were not, and are not, abstractions. These are the neighbors and friends and family of everyone in New Orleans—and, by extension, in the United States. The expression "There but for the grace of God go I" has fallen into some disuse recently, but it is useful, whatever your God looks like. The person who suffers *is* you.

Anger is famous for being, often, a mask for profound grief. As we watched the disgracefully slow and inadequate federal, state, and local response, the horrible conditions the people of New Orleans, our people, had to endure, the anger was debilitating, but slowly the grief became overwhelming. Eighty percent of the city, according to most reports, had flooded. Not necessarily to the rooftops in all places, but enough to ruin homes, businesses, and . . . and . . .

Yes: *and*. If one took one's eyes off the maddening images on the television, one began to think of other images, of the city one knew and recognized, lived in and loved the way you love a person. New Orleans inspires the kind of love that very few other cities do. Paris, maybe Venice, maybe, San Francisco, New York. . . . The list is not that much longer. New Orleans has a mythology, a personality, a *soul,* that is large, and that has touched people around the world. It has its own music (many of its own musics), its own cuisine, its own way of talking, its own architecture, its own smell, its own look and feel.

I write "has" instead of "had," even though at the moment of this writing it is hard to imagine how the city can come back not just from the natural blows, the material and economic damage, but also the human, spiritual blows that it has sustained and continues to sustain. But it is just not natural to speak of New Orleans in the past tense. There is an element about it that is timeless, that is always the present.

The past in New Orleans cohabits with the present to an extent not even approximated in any other North American city. Walking through the Tulane University campus, way uptown, you can see the old gymnasium where King Oliver's Creole Jazz band, with a young Louis Armstrong on cornet, played for dances. If you are adventuresome, and you know where to go, you can find the houses of Jelly Roll Morton and Buddy Bolden and Papa Jack Laine and the rest of the earliest generation of jazz musicians. In the French Quarter you can cut out of Jackson Square, ringed by the Pontalba Apartments, the oldest apartment buildings in North America, walk down nar-

row Pirate's Alley where Jean Lafitte used to hang out, between St. Louis Cathedral on your right and the huge
bulk of the Cabildo on your left, at one time the seat of
Spanish government in the territory and the place where
the Louisiana Purchase was signed, and half a block down
encounter a great bookstore in the house where William
Faulkner wrote his first novel, *Soldier's Pay*. A few blocks
away, Tennessee Williams lived and wrote, amid scenes
made famous by Walker Percy, George W. Cable, and
other writers too numerous to mention.

These elements of New Orleans possess an astonishing vitality that has spoken to people around the world
and shaped much of the best of what we think of still as
American culture. Jazz music, rhythm and blues, and rock
and roll, Creole cooking, Mardi Gras, the architecture of
the French Quarter, the literary traditions of Williams and
Faulkner and Percy and Kate Chopin, the Mardi Gras
Indians, whose chanted songs stretch back into the nineteenth century and whose rhythms help form the basis of
American popular music. . . . It is not something that you
find only in a tourist guide; it is a reality lived by its in-
habitants every day, and as often as possible by those who
love visiting.

It is also a city with enormous problems even on its

best day. A friend told me of a conversation she had had with an Australian journalist in which she had begun enumerating some of those problems—terrible poverty and hard living conditions for so many of the residents, often within a block of opulent mansions, one of the highest murder and crime rates in the nation, public schools falling apart physically and socially, a police department that in some seasons can be scarier than the city's criminals, official corruption at every level, not to mention weather that for at least seven months a year is equivalent to wearing a towel soaked in steaming hot water wrapped around your head.

The Australian listened to the list with mounting alarm, finally saying, "My God, it sounds like a horrible place to live."

"Are you kidding?" my friend said. "It's a *great* place to live!"

Everyone who loves New Orleans learns to love it with its flaws. It may be hard for people who have never been to the Crescent City to understand the passionate love people have for it, to understand why it's worth fighting for—why it *matters*. There would be so many things to explain, and so many of them are visible only between the lines. You would have to show them the St. Charles Avenue streetcar rolling slowly along its track in the morning haze under the avenue's great oak trees, past some of the most beautiful houses in America, or a second-line parade in which everyone following the brass band (and the brightly costumed members of this or that Social Aid and Pleasure Club) dance intricate steps through the streets of the neighborhood where they grew up, or you could show them a Mardi Gras Indian practice. You could bring them to zydeco night at Rock 'n' Bowl, where a live band plays for dancers up on the mezzanine level while people bowl happily a few feet away, or to Snug Harbor to hear Ellis Marsalis play piano, or you could even sit them down at one of those cramped counters at Central Grocery and put half a muffuletta sandwich and a Barq's root beer in front of them, or give them a Pimm's Cup at the Napoleon House, or best of all, some of the fried chicken at Willie Mae's Scotch House across from the Lafitte projects.

Even then, the meaning is between the lines. New Orleans is not just a list of attractions or restaurants or ceremonies, no matter how sublime and subtle. New Orleans is the interaction among all those things, and countless more. It gains its character from the spirit that is summoned, like a hologram, in the midst of all these elements, and that comes, ultimately, from the people who live there—those who have chosen to live there, and those whose parents and grandparents and ancestors lived there.

That spirit, as much as, or more than, the city's physical and economic infrastructure, is what is in jeopardy right now. In the wake of the worst natural disaster in this country's history, one from which New Orleans, and the rest of the country, will be digging out for years, it may be good to remember what has been lost, and to think hard about what is worth fighting to save.

That is what this book is about.

# PART I

# 1.

Long before I visited New Orleans I would visit it in my imagination. I would strain to see it through the small windows of the photos in the books that I took out from the library when I was barely into my teens—*A Pictorial History of Jazz, Shining Trumpets, Jazzmen*—graying black-and-white pictures of men with musical instruments, seated for formal band portraits or playing on a bandstand somewhere, or even marching through the streets. The streets were lined with wooden frame houses, apparently unpainted, and little shops and bars whose roofs stretched out over the sidewalks and seemed to lean a little to one side, casting deep shadows, with names like Luthjen's, Big 25, Mama Lou's.

In the formal portraits the men were dressed in their band uniforms, looking proudly straight at the camera.

They seemed to know that they were worth something. They often held their instruments with a little flair, at a certain angle, never as if an afterthought or an appendage, but somehow as the point of their presence there.

Often the photos were scratchy, the only copy of an image fixed near the beginning of the twentieth century—but they contained such power. Today, of course, images are reproduced digitally ad infinitum, and we are drowning in them; they have in many ways lost their value, even become part of the problem—a logjam, a glut of disconnected information. But these older images were powerful and unique, often showing fold marks or tears; they had been smuggled out of the past as if containing an important message that the past wanted us to know. Whoever had held onto them had wanted them to endure.

It was the same with the early recordings of New Orleans jazz. They sounded different from the other records I listened to in the sixties—not the actual music, although that was different enough, but the sound quality. The sound was a primitive monaural, more contained, and often there was a sonic drizzle of scratchy surface noise through which the music reached out. You had to reach back to it, make an effort, to get its message, and that was part of the experience. It demanded an investment on your part; you had to, in a sense, complete the picture.

But once you had learned how to reach out and get the message, it got easier and more natural, and you began to want to spend more time over there, where the message was. The beauty and mystery and intelligence that waited for you, like an unknown continent to explore. The Louis Armstrong Hot Fives, Jelly Roll Morton's Red Hot Peppers, King Oliver's Creole Jazz Band—and, later, Fats Domino, and Professor Longhair and Irma Thomas and Dr. John, and so many others.

Music was my entry point into the world of the spirit that New Orleans embodies. But there are so many other possible entry points, too—culinary, social, historical, literary, and architectural—all of them connected. For years, because of what I heard in the music, I wanted to visit that place. Eventually, after many visits, I ended up moving there. Today I travel a lot, and when I tell people that I live in New Orleans their expression changes slightly; something in their facial muscles relaxes, something brightens in their eyes, and they smile.

When I finally did visit for the first time, almost

twenty years ago, years before I moved there, I began to
see that the music I loved was just one facet of a kind of
unified field of culture, of *being*. You sensed it as soon as
you entered the city. The air smelled different; it felt different, heavier, on your arms, more like a liquid than like
air. After New York City, where I lived and which I also
loved, with its sharp right angles and hard surfaces and fast
tempo and endless pavement and soaring vertical walls, a
giant video game of the mind at the expense of the body,
New Orleans was like finding yourself in some electri-
cally charged soup. People said hello when they passed
you on the street, and after a few days you started saying
hello back to them. The fragrant bushes were an endless
olfactory ambush in the evenings—sweet olive and ligus-
trum and Confederate jasmine. You could get stunningly
great food even in tiny and sometimes dingy corner bars,
as well as in an endless array of neighborhood restaurants, like Domilise's, or Mandina's, or Willie Mae's, or
Uglesich's, often tucked back in a residential block somewhere, each of which seemed to have its own particular
culinary groove going.

Then there was music, which could arrive anywhere, at any time. Your car would be held up at an inter-
section for no apparent reason, and you would be

wondering what in God's name the problem might be, and then you would hear the trumpets off in the distance, then the rest of the horns, the tubas and the drums, amid the shouts and laughter of the celebrants as they passed (or the mourners, if it was a jazz funeral), and you would pull your car over and lock it and follow the parade for as long as it took you to remember that you were supposed to be someplace twenty minutes ago.

New Orleans wasn't something I was able to brush off lightly, and I went back every chance I got. I left New York in 1991 to attend the Iowa Writers' Workshop, and when I was finished with Iowa I decided to move to New Orleans. It was cheaper than New York, and I wanted to be writing fiction rather than scrambling just to make rent money, and I had always wanted to live there anyway. I moved to New Orleans in 1994 and soon knew that it was home, for keeps, no matter where I might travel.

You can find the city's official history elsewhere, how it was founded in 1718 by Jean Baptiste La Moyne and became the provincial capital of the French colony of Louisiana. You can read how Jean Lafitte and Andrew Jackson and Thomas Jefferson handled themselves while in town, and how the French and the Spanish wrangled there, and then how it became an infamous center of the

slave trade, to the extent that even today the small out-
buildings off the courtyards in back of all those pictur-
esque houses in the French Quarter are called "slave
quarters" with pride by realtors. They are quite a drawing
card for the properties that have them. You can read about
who built the Pontalba Apartments, and Jackson Square,
and St. Louis Cathedral. You can read how and why the
city spread both uptown and down, how it is organized
into wards, and who built it and made all the money for
the people who owned it—the carpenters and masons and
plasterers and stoneworkers and wrought-iron workers
and strongbacks and, later, the plumbers and electricians,
the stained-glass artisans and the engineers who designed
the levees, and the riverboat people and the restaurant
people and the brewers and the sugar cane people and
later the oil people and, always, the musicians, the ones
who play in the street for tips and the ones who play in
the street for parades, and the ones who play in the fancy
hotels and the dive bars and nightclubs and also the ones
who just play for their own damn selves whenever they
feel like it, and all the rest who made that beautiful city—
the Irish and the Italians and the Africans and the Haitians
and the Croatians and the Portuguese and the Cape
Verdeans and the Polish and everybody else in the family.

You will have to read that elsewhere, because this isn't a history book. It is a book about the things that have evolved parallel to the city's history. Along the way some history will have to be brought in, because after all some hard and sad facts are necessary to understanding some parts of it. But history is what has passed, and this is a book about what is and must continue to be. Every place has its history, but what is it about New Orleans that makes it more than just the sum of the events that have happened there? What gives it a meaning and a soul so that it is known throughout the world as a place to visit to revive the spirit? What is it about the spirit of the people who live there that could produce a music, a cuisine, an architecture, a total environment, the mere mention of which can bring a smile to the face of someone who has never even set foot there?

What is the meaning of a place like that, and what is lost if it is lost?

# 2.

I first visited the Crescent City, named for the curve of the Mississippi River into which it is nestled, in 1987, for the annual New Orleans Jazz and Heritage Festival, universally referred to as Jazz Fest. I had been planning to make the trip for years and had always put off the visit for one reason or another, usually having to do with not having any money. That January, coming off the long and painful breakup of a relationship, I attended a party thrown to help everyone through the final grinding weeks of a long New York City winter. Someone mentioned to me that he was going to Jazz Fest, which always takes place on the last weekend in April and the first weekend in May.

"Why don't you go?" he said. "Think of the spiritual renewal."

I began to offer my usual excuses about dwindling funds and taxes coming due. My friend looked me in the eye and said, "Go into debt."

It was the best advice anyone had ever given me. As time went on, I learned that this is a very New Orleans attitude, for good and ill.

When you go to New Orleans—as when you go to Paris—people fall over themselves recommending favorite restaurants, bars, neighborhoods, music clubs, lunch joints, record stores, book shops, streets, activities. One friend of mine in particular, a New Orleans native transplanted to New York, gave me a list of places to go—the Napoleon House (make sure and drink a Pimm's Cup), the Camellia Grill (get either the pecan waffles or the chili cheese omelet), Central Grocery (best muffuletta), Tipitina's, the Maple Leaf Bar, Lafitte's Blacksmith Shop, the Port of Call, Sid-Mar's, Bruning's. . . . The names of the places themselves, and the streets where they were located—St. Louis, Decatur, Esplanade, Perdido, Frenchmen—sounded mysterious and poetic to my ears, which were used to the numbered grid of New York City.

The guest house where I was staying, booked through some fly-by-night accommodations agency I had stumbled across, was in a beautiful area that I only later found out was supposed to be dangerous, the lovely, shaded stretch of Prytania Street in the neighborhood where streets are named for the Muses—Euterpe, Melpomene, Terpsichore, and Polymnia—one block off of St. Charles Avenue with its streetcar, and walking distance from Lee Circle.

If the Addams Family had run a guest house, it would have looked something like Longpre Gardens—a narrow Victorian wooden frame house with peeling blue paint, sagging porch, rusted, knee-high iron fence, scraggly weeds in the patch of yard between sidewalk and front door. When my host answered the door, he looked me up and down with a raised eyebrow and a muted, arch smile, welcomed me in and informed me that due to a scheduling overlap, my room was occupied by someone else. I would be welcome to sleep on the one available cot, either in the kitchen or—a significant pause—in his room.

Standing there in the gloomy, high-ceilinged, musty entry hall, I had an overwhelming impulse to get a cab back to the airport and return to New York City. This was going to be my spiritual renewal? Sleeping on a cot and fighting off the advances of this sweetnatured old queen? Nothing personal to him, but that wasn't my thing, and anyway I had wanted a place of comfort and restoration, not a makeshift bed in a kitchen.

I tried to process it. I had wanted to come to New Orleans for a long, long time, since I was a kid, and now I was here. There were places I wanted to see, and I wouldn't be spending that much time at the guest house anyway. I had been fighting my own life for months, wishing things were different from how they were, and I had made a sacrifice to come to a place where I thought they would be the way I wanted them to be, and now it turned out to be different from what I had expected. I just wanted to be somewhere, for a while, where things were okay just the way they were.

And then, somehow, a switch clicked inside me, some spirit of place must have entered me, and I thought: Why not declare that, as of now, things are okay just as they are? While you are here, declare things okay as they are. Take what comes.

I thanked my host for the choice and told him I would take the kitchen.

I didn't know it consciously at that point, but I had stepped into one of the most important lessons that New Orleans offers: Go with what *is.* Use what happens. Years later, attending second-line parades as they moved through all the neighborhoods, I would see this principle embodied in dancers who incorporate all the small accidents of geography—lightpoles, fire hydrants, cars—into their ongoing improvised dance. It was in fact the spirit of Mardi Gras itself, when for one day everyone in the city decides to go with whatever happens. But I'm getting ahead of things.

As soon as I adjusted to the reality (the private room miraculously became available the next day), I got out into the city. The first thing I did was rent a bicycle on Frenchmen Street in the Faubourg Marigny, which is to the French Quarter what New York's East Village is to Greenwich Village proper. New Orleans is a great city for bicycling; there are no hills to speak of, so it never becomes an athletic event. There is an extremely active street life and sidewalk life; people like to sit on their porches and talk, stop friends on street corners for a chat, unexpected parades. The streets themselves are small masterpieces of intrigue and grace, with names that invite you in—Story, Music, Desire, and Harmony—and each has its own distinct personality. And of course there was the French Quarter to look forward to, with its Burgundy Street and Bourbon Street.

I biked everywhere on that trip. I rode from the

Marigny out broad Elysian Fields all the way to Lake
Pontchartrain, a long ride in itself, then along the lake
shore to Bucktown and back down, skirting City Park and
burrowing through all the neighborhoods along Carrolton Avenue, finally coming out by the Mississippi River
levee at the foot of Carrolton, and rolling down St.
Charles Avenue in the afternoon shade. There was such
variety in the neighborhoods—rich or poor, shaded or
bare. But they also had something in common, a kind of
frequency to which they were tuned, different as they may
have been. Always there was some kind of sign of gratitude for the fact of being there, whether it was lovely
landscaping under beautiful trees in the Garden District,
or a couch placed on a porch in one of the poorest neighborhoods, with a scraggly potted palm next to it and a
man seated there raising his drink in salute as I passed.
There was a sense of welcome, a sense of appreciation of
being alive. The only place where this wasn't immediately
recognizable was in the one or two housing projects that I
passed—prefabricated, gloomy places with burned-out
looking windows that stared like dead eyes and doors
open to dark hallways. But even there, I would learn, people found a way to make life livable.

★  ★  ★

The first meal I ate in New Orleans was at an unpromising-looking corner place a couple of blocks from the guest house. I approached it philosophically: I was hungry, it was close, and at least it wasn't a chain. When the fried trout arrived and I tasted it, I had trouble believing how good it was. It tasted both of the fish, which was fresh, and of some judiciously wielded seasoning that I couldn't identify, and the greens that came with it had small pieces of bacon the flavor of which suffused the dish. This in a place that somewhere else might have served fare that was mediocre at best. I actually laughed out loud. The next morning I went back there for breakfast and had eggs and grits and smoked sausage and confirmed my previous night's estimate of the place.

New Orleans, as everyone knows, takes its food seriously. And food is tied up with all the rhythms of life in the city. Aside from the Catholic penchant for fish on Fridays, there is also the tradition of eating red beans and rice on Monday (Monday was traditionally wash day; fishermen did not work on Sundays, and in the days before refrigeration beans and rice was a slow-cooking, fishless meal that could simmer while the laundry was being done), and various neighborhood mini-traditions, often associated with Friday and the end of the work week, such as the long-standing Kermit Ruffins barbecue fest at Vaughan's low-slung corner joint down in the Bywater, or the long liquid lunch at Galatoire's.

As in Paris, visitors tend to map out their visits around favorite restaurants and tend not to feel they have really arrived in town until they've had that baked ham po-boy at Mother's, or Paul's Fantasy at Uglesich's, or a muffuletta at Central Grocery or the Napoleon House, to speak only of lunch stops. I would have added fried chicken at Willie Mae's Scotch House, but until very recently that was a stop known only to neighborhood folks and a select handful of others. Then Willie Mae—a diminutive eighty-eight-year-old lady with a hairnet who still cooks all the fried chicken herself, standing in suffocating heat in the kitchen of her little corner store restaurant with five or six tables in it, where her great-granddaughter waits tables—went to New York City in the spring of 2005 to receive an America's Classic Award from the James Beard Foundation, and Willie Mae's got added to the Out Of Town Hipster Visitor List. Six months later, during Hurricane Katrina, it flooded to the roof.

There are the great restaurants that have made names for themselves known around the world—Antoine's and Brennan's, Bayona and Commander's Palace, and Gala-toire's, Emeril's, Bacco, NOLA, Peristyle, and newer entries such as Cobalt, and Herbsaint. Then there are restaurants that are more local to certain parts of the city, and which have loyal clientele and still serve world-class food, like the Upperline, or Brigtsen's, or Gautreau's, Feelings, Pampy's, Irene's, Café Degas, Sid-Mar's, Bruning's, Manditch, Casa-mento's, Clancy's, or Crescent City Steak House out on Broad Street, where you can sit in one of the tiny wooden booths from the John Garfield days with a curtain that closes. These places just mentioned are dotted throughout the city—Uptown, Bucktown, Bayou St. John, Mid-City, Bywater, Upper Ninth Ward. And of course there is Mosca's, which is not technically in New Orleans proper, being twenty minutes' drive across the river through the reaches of the West Bank, a tiny place stuck by the side of the road out in the middle of nowhere, but one of New Orleans's great places anyway, everything served family style—oysters roasted in a pan with seasoned bread-crumbs, and chicken cacciatore with a rosemary sauce that is so good that you can, and will, use a second loaf of their delicious bread just to soak up the sauce from the pan.

But the real neighborhood places, tucked away usually in some unlikely corner of a residential street, animate the day-to-day grass roots culinary life of the city. There is nothing fancy or elaborate about these places to say the least, but also nothing humdrum or mass-produced, or even lackluster, as I found out on that first evening. It is a point of honor to make food that tastes good—I don't think a New Orleanian would even understand the concept of turning out blah food so you could just eat and run. You can go into the most unassuming place—say, Domilise's, a sandwich shop with a hand-lettered sign in a very modest corner house a block from the river in a residential uptown neighborhood—and get a meal that you will remember for the rest of your days. Or at least for the rest of the day. These kinds of places each have their own personality—Dunbar's, with its great fried chicken, Liuzza's, where until recently they still featured a dish on the menu called Wop Salad, Garce's Cuban joint back behind Rock 'n' Bowl, Manuel's Hot Tamales, right on Carrolton—walk up and they'll give you as many as you want, wrapped in newspaper—or Mandina's, or Parasol's, or the St. Charles Tavern, or the Clover Grill. And don't start talking about all the snowball stands—snowballs being shaved ice suffused with any one of a hundred different flavored sugary syrups—like Hansen's, or Plum Street Snowballs, half a block from my house, or Angelo Brocato's great Italian ice cream parlor in Mid-City. Or the institution of the crawfish boil, for which folks gather at a friend's house where an outdoor table is covered with newspaper and hundreds of boiled crawfish are dumped out along with the potatoes and corn on the cob that have been boiled along with them, and everyone eats and drinks beer until the host passes out and everyone straggles home.

Many of the restaurants just mentioned, which their partisans love with the kind of love often reserved for a dear friend, were flooded or otherwise damaged during Hurricane Katrina. Others may or may not have been; the picture, as I write this, is still incomplete. It seems possible that a place like Casamento's, on Magazine Street, which is a sacred temple with shiny tiled walls, dedicated to oysters raw, fried and stewed, might not survive, if only because the local shellfish industry may have been dealt a lethal blow by the spread of the toxic floodwaters; it will be quite a while before the impact of the flooding is accurately assessed. Mandina's and Liuzza's, and Brocato's, and Manuel's are located in a section of Mid-City where the flooding was severe, and their businesses may not survive. To anyone who loves New Orleans, this is as heart-breaking as the shattering of the stained-glass windows at Sainte-Chappelle would be to those who love Paris.

These are not just isolated places where people dine and whose demise is regrettable but which are essentially replaceable by something else, no more than the death of one of your siblings can be shrugged off. Each of these restaurants is, in all its idiosyncrasy, part of a larger fabric, a culture of food, but whose meaning extends beyond food, as may be said of almost all aspects of New Orleans culture. A family is a culture, a language is a culture, and the food of New Orleans is a language, and those who prepare it and love it are a family.

Food in New Orleans is rarely a means to an end. It is an end in itself, and one in which the participants are emotionally invested. As with New Orleans music, it is part of a shared ritual in which life itself is appreciated and honored in all its specificity and variety, its thereness. It is not the master-and-commander relationship to food of the wine taster, the distanced, appraising relation of the food critic (although so much of it would stand up to the toughest appraisal)—it is the passionate, grateful, sacra-mental relationship of a kind of nonsectarian communion. You are free to believe this or not, but those who have experienced it know it is true.

If all of it sounds vaguely religious, I would say that it isn't that vague. New Orleans is the most religious place I have ever been, even though much of the population is profoundly profane, pagan, and steeped in the seven deadly sins and some others not even listed.

Beyond the obvious and close connections between music and dance in New Orleans, there is a close relationship as well between music and food. "Music begins to atrophy," wrote Ezra Pound in his *ABC of Reading*, "when it departs too far from the dance." In New Orleans, music begins to atrophy when it departs too far from food. The titles of so many tunes are themselves a clue—Louis Armstrong's "Struttin' with Some Barbecue," Professor Longhair's "Crawfish Fiesta" and "Red Beans," "Low Gravy" by Jelly Roll Morton and his Red Hot Peppers. Trumpeter Kermit Ruffins as often as not will set up his barbecue rig and cook up a mess of sausages and turkey necks outside a club where he is playing a gig.

Rarely is the best New Orleans music found in a

concert hall where the audience sits separated from the performers by a proscenium, listening politely and then applauding at the end of each selection. It happens, but it isn't New Orleans at its most identifiable. New Orleans music lovers, black, white, young and old, are much more likely to be found in places where they can dance to the music they love, holler encouragement, sing along and, if at all possible, eat and drink at the same time. If that can happen in a concert hall, fine, but it is much more likely to happen in a bar or a club, often with windows open onto the street, or even—perhaps even most often—on the street itself. In almost every New Orleans club, the life of the club spills out onto the street. It doesn't matter if it's barnlike Tipitina's under the oak trees and a block from the railroad tracks at Napoleon and Tchoupitoulas, or Kemp's Lounge, across from what is now called A. L. Davis Park, but which all residents, characteristically, call by its old name, Shakespeare Park, or the pressed-tin-lined Maple Leaf Bar up on Oak Street, where James Booker used to wring unbelievable sounds out of one of the worst pianos ever destroyed by the hands of man, or the old Glass House, or Vaughan's, or long-gone and much beloved Little People's in the Treme. You will find folks outside listening to the sounds from inside, taking a break from all the heat and noise, having a few laughs and talking with friends old and new.

Mac Rebennack, better known as Dr. John, once told me that when a brass band plays at a small club back up in one of the neighborhoods, it's as if the audience—dancing, singing to the refrains, laughing—is part of the band. They are two parts of the same thing. The dancers interpret, or it might be better to say literally embody, the sounds of the band, answering the instruments. Since everyone is listening to different parts of the music—she to the trumpet melody, he to the bass drum, she to the trombone—the audience is a working model in three dimensions of the music, a synesthesic transformation of materials. And of course the band is also watching the dancers, and getting ideas from the dancers' gestures. The relationship between band and audience is in that sense like the relationship between two lovers making love, where cause and effect becomes very hard to see, even impossible to call by its right name; one is literally *getting down*, as in particle physics, to some root stratum where one is freed from the lockstep of time itself, where time might even run backward, or sideways, and something eternal and transcendent is accessed.

This is of course the function of all ritual, in one

way or another—to short-circuit time in its dumb, earth-bound mortal sequence, and restate the things that will last and constantly renew the world. Nowhere is this more visible than in the famous New Orleans tradition of jazz funerals. In its most boiled-down form, such funerals—usually held for community leaders or well known musicians, or for members of the city's many Social Aid and Pleasure Clubs, with names like the Moneywasters and the Treme Sports and the Scene Boosters and the Zulu Social Aid and Pleasure Club, which pool their money for such occasions—consist of a long church service, usually itself containing music, a sermon or sermons, and spoken reminiscences, which is followed by a ritual that stretches back well over a hundred years.

After all is done inside the church, the pall bearers, dressed impeccably in suits, carry the remains of the departed outside and place them usually into a traditional horse-drawn carriage, with the driver sitting atop, dressed in a somber tuxedo with a black top hat; the family may ride behind it in the sleekest of air-conditioned limousines, but the body itself goes in the carriage.

Outside on the street will be a crowd, often numbering in the hundreds, of friends who couldn't get into the church, or who didn't want to have to sit still for two

hours in the sweltering heat, or people who were only ac-
quaintances of the deceased, or people who had only
heard of the deceased, or people who didn't know him at
all (most jazz funerals seem to be for men) but knew there
was going to be a funeral, or people who just happen to
live on the block or nearby blocks and came to hear the
band and participate, or who just happened to find themselves on the sidewalk on a sunny morning in a ragged
T-shirt and beat-up baseball cap with the bill turned to
the side, a little red-eyed and worse for wear, wearing a
smile and ready to toast their unknown brother's depar-
ture to Glory. Down on the corner someone is probably
cooking up barbecued chicken in a converted oil drum
on the back of a pickup truck, and others have beer and
sweet wine on ice in portable coolers.

The word that the body is coming out usually precedes the body by several minutes, and the crowd seems to
get denser, hotter; the sun beats down on everyone's heads
except those who brought umbrellas (used much more in
New Orleans for sun than for rain). When the church's
doors open and the pallbearers bring the body out, dea-
cons or funeral officials will tell the crowd to clear back a
little, which it will do with some effort as the bodies are
all pressed together, and the brass band, which has been

waiting, will start playing a slow, wailing dirge. Slowly the men carry the casket to the back of the waiting carriage—the same carriage that is, literally or figuratively, awaiting everybody on that street, someday. As the casket is slid in, the trumpet will be playing the melody of a hymn, usually "Just A Closer Walk With Thee" (in the old days the brass bands had a wider repertoire of hymns; you might have heard "Flee as a Bird," or "Old Rugged Cross" or any number of others) and the trombone will be answering, and the clarinets, and the tuba, while the bass drum emits a slow, low thump and the snare drum plays a stately, slow beat.

This takes a while to do, and it would take an artist like Brueghel, or Daumier, to capture the simultaneous modes occurring on the street—the curious people pushing in, expressionless, to watch and catch a glimpse, thinking about their own death maybe, or that of someone they knew, or maybe just thinking about the previous night's episode of *American Idol;* across the street folks from the neighborhood laughing and telling jokes on the front steps of their houses that face right up on the sidewalk, doors open to the dark interiors, next to little groupings of the music and culture lovers from other areas who come to pay homage to the tradition itself, some watching and taking it all in, some catching up on gossip from the music business, or the academic folklore biz, while out of the church across the street pour the well-wishers, the family, the grief-struck, and, doubtless, those who never liked that dead motherfucker one little bit but who needed to attend for one reason or another.

When the back of the carriage is closed and secured, everyone takes up their positions and the procession commences, usually with the band leading the way in front of the carriage and, if it's a big enough funeral, another band bringing up the rear, and the whole procession begins moving slowly through the crowded street, with the trumpets playing the melody of the dirge, the trombones wailing their responses, the high clarinets playing countermelodies or harmonies, the tubas anchoring everything with their low notes and the drums playing in time, the snare drum muffled (in the old days the snare drummer would play with a folded handkerchief to muffle the sound of the sticks as they struck the drum). Behind them are the official pallbearers and ushers, and anyone else who wants to be part of the procession, walking slowly, often doing a little stop-time step in time to the snare drum's little catch-rhythm. They wear officially sorrowful expressions, and some of them are no doubt sorrowful inside as well, but in the most profound sense it is a masque of grief that is being staged here, in which the fact of mortality is being given its due, and yet is also undercut by what is about to happen.

In the real old times they would continue this way all the way to the graveyard before the next stage of the funeral ritual took place, but even New Orleans isn't totally immune to the Worldwide Attention Deficit, and today this part of the procession will last for a block or two at most before the band stops playing the dirge (in the old times the snare drummer would, at this point, remove the handkerchief from the head of the snare drum) and the snare drum beats out a familiar sharp tattoo, the band launches into a jubilant, life-affirming stomp, and the entire crowd explodes into dance.

The procession keeps rolling, followed now by some of the greatest dancing you have ever seen. Some follow the parade, smiling and holding up their cans of beer, waving to friends, or with their arms around their friends, some executing incredibly intricate steps by themselves as they move along, up onto the sidewalk, around cars, back onto the street, or in duet with someone else, trying to outdo each other, never for very long until they split up and find someone else; people are dancing on porches and steps as the parade passes; members of the parade will climb up on light poles and dumpsters and even the roofs of cars (don't park along a funeral route if you can help it), dancing to the music in celebration of the fact that, cold as it may sound, it isn't their time yet to be inside that carriage. They know it is coming, and that is a large part of why they dance. The parade will wind through the streets of the neighborhood, usually passing by beloved watering holes known or unknown to the deceased, where all may partake of a little liquid sacrament, wish the departed a good journey to the land of the shades, and then continue rolling, sometimes for hours.

So which is real, the grief or the celebration? Both, simultaneously, and that is why it is profound. You might sometimes see a mother dancing behind a casket containing the body of her own dead son, with tears of grief running down her face. Most funeral traditions in our society are there to remind us that we are dust, and to dust we shall return. In New Orleans the funerals remind us that Life is bigger than any individual life, and it will roll on, and for the short time that your individual life joins the big stream of Life, cut some decent steps, for God's sake. No individual life lasts forever, and it is the responsibility of those left outside the walls of the boneyard to keep life going. This isn't escapism, or denial of grief; it is

acceptance of the facts of life, the map of a profound relationship to the grief that is a part of life, and it will tell
you something about why the real New Orleans spirit is
never silly, or never just silly, in celebration, and never
maudlin in grief. Under ordinary circumstances the word
"irony" might come to mind, but the detachment implied
by that word doesn't seem to quite fit the situation. It is a
way of containing the opposites that are a part of life in a
way that allows the individual, and the community, to
function with style and grace, even wit, under the most
adverse circumstances.

(It has nothing to do with the vulgar caricature of
this spirit offered on Bourbon Street to the casual visitor,
a version of the culture where the most obvious elements
are exaggerated and the subtleties erased.)


New Orleans culture is of a piece. You can't really lose
one part of it without losing the whole thing. The music
is part of the parades, and the basis of the dancing that you
see, or do, at the parades. The parades are part of the
rhythms of the year, and of life—the anniversaries, holidays, birthdays, and funerals. They wind through the
streets of the neighborhoods where people live; they stop

for refreshment in the tiny corner bars where people drink and pass the time, and at day's end, after all the parading, people settle down to familiar food like red beans and rice, or crawfish, or stuffed mirliton or shrimp creole or oysters, with the music and the dancing and all the things that happened still ringing in them, and that is part of the whole package, too. It amounts to a kind of cultural synesthesia in which music is food, and food is a kind of choreography, and dance is a way of dramatizing the fact that you are still alive for another year, another funeral, another Mardi Gras. This is true at all levels of the society, but the maintaining and restating of that fact is a matter of spiritual life and death especially among the city's poorest African American residents, among whom so many of New Orleans's most recognized and important cultural expressions arose in the first place.

It is tempting to say that if you are talking about the spirit you are talking about something that cannot die. But the spirit can be broken, and killed. It can even die of neglect. In Judeo-Christian traditions the spirit comes from an independent God who is beyond time, whose existence, if that is the word, precedes that of mankind and will outlast it. New Orleans is largely Catholic, so it pays lip service to this paradigm through its institutionally sanctioned religious rituals, but in practice the real belief is probably closer to the African-based religious systems in which the Gods live only when incarnate in human action. A ritual space is established, and individuals in the rituals act as vehicles for divine spirits; they literally make the Gods, give life to the Gods, because without the Gods their own lives are meaningless. And without incarnation, the Gods are, at best, incomplete. It is a form of consummation.

Catholicism, with its devotion not just to the Holy Trinity but to the Virgin Mary and all the Saints, who are seen as intercessors and even divinities in their own right, has often been conflated with these African-based religions, in Cuba, in Haiti and other places where Spanish and French conquerors took over people with roots in Africa, including New Orleans. Each saint is seen as the patron saint of something—travel, the sick, fishermen— and has his or her own mythology and life narrative and special powers and interests. They are kept alive in memory and spirit by special devotion, by prayer and observance, often by sacrifice.

In New Orleans this attitude or inclination is hardly the exclusive property of those whose ancestral roots go back to Africa. The Irish paraders celebrate St. Patrick's

Day by throwing cabbages to roadside celebrants. The city's old-line Italians celebrate St. Joseph's Day for a week beforehand by making "St. Joseph's altars," on which food of all description is piled high in homes and at churches; people come in to view and comment on the altars and give donations to the church; at the end the food is donated to charity. Black New Orleans celebrates St. Joseph, too, with Indians taking to the streets and roaming all over town on St. Joseph's Night.

New Orleanians, poor, rich, and in-between, white and black and in-between, take their cooking and eating seriously, just as they take their music seriously, and their dancing, and their masks and costumes, and their celebratory rituals, because it is not mere entertainment to them. It is all part of a ritual in which the finiteness, the specificity and fragility and durability and richness and earthiness and sadness and laughter of life, are all mixed together, honored, and given tangible form in sound, movement, and communal cuisine.

It is a religious attitude, but it is not the stern Calvinist religion of judgment and renunciation of New England, nor does it have anything in common with some virulent new strains of fundamentalism in which the fondest hope is that Our God, whatever His name is,

Blessed Be His Name, will come and Really Kick Some Ass and wipe away all the crud and leave only the elect. Nor does it have anything to do with the false and obscene pieties mouthed by those for whom Jesus is just another means to get power and votes and government contracts. Its fruits are given freely, in an expression and an imitation of the generosity of creation itself, and very often by the humblest people in the community. But it is appreciated by all who have ears to hear and eyes to see and tongues to taste and hearts to love. And once you love you cannot turn your back.

# 3.

Where would you start with New Orleans music? Where would you end? Everyone everywhere knows that jazz music was born in New Orleans. But, beyond that, all American music in the twentieth century was profoundly shaped and influenced by New Orleans music—that is, all American music that was not itself New Orleans music.

You could start with Jelly Roll Morton's historic 1938 recordings for the Library of Congress, made under the supervision of the legendary folklorist Alan Lomax. By coincidence they were issued, complete and remastered, on eight compact discs in a boxed set, in the weeks immediately following Hurricane Katrina. In them, jazz's first composer, one of its best pianists, and one of its most flamboyant characters, tells the story of his youth in late nineteenth-century New Orleans, talks of the hustlers and gamblers and musicians, the famous red light district Storyville, and then of his own subsequent travels and adventures; his stories are interspersed with, and often accompanied by, his own piano playing. These recordings are the Dead Sea Scrolls of jazz, fascinating as musicology, historiography, and flat-out storytelling.

Or maybe you could start with *The Atlantic New Orleans Jazz Sessions.* These discs, originally recorded in the 1950s and early 1960s, show brass bands playing in a style that was probably entirely representative of early street music. It includes a recording of the Young Tuxedo Brass Band playing a complete funeral procession—from dirge to celebratory stomps—recorded live in the New Orleans streets. Or you can listen to the first jazz recordings ever made, from 1917, by the Original Dixieland Jazz Band, full of gusto and fun, and including the first recorded versions of tunes such as "Tiger Rag," "Sensation Rag," and "Original Dixieland One-Step," or the great early recordings by the New Orleans Rhythm Kings with clarinetist Leon Rappolo.

But certainly the recordings of King Oliver's Creole Jazz Band, from 1923 and 1924, with a very young Louis Armstrong on cornet playing next to his mentor Oliver, are the high-water mark of early recorded New Orleans jazz. The Oliver band brought the classic New Orleans approach—in which the trumpet or cornet plays variations on the melody, the trombone plays shorter answering and harmony phrases, and the clarinet provides a filigreed descant—to its first and greatest flowering: four different horns (Oliver and Armstrong both played simultaneous melodic variations) all playing different lines, with such soul and humor and swing, like listening to improvised Bach counterpoint.

Jelly Roll Morton's own small-band performances, recorded beginning in 1926 under the name Jelly Roll Morton's Red Hot Peppers, constitute the only other body of work in New Orleans Jazz that fully equals Oliver's. While the Creole Jazz Band gave maximum freedom to each member (within carefully defined boundaries), Morton liked his musicians to play exactly what he wrote. Recordings such as "Black Bottom Stomp," "Dead Man Blues" (with its evocation of a New Orleans funeral), "Kansas City Stomps," "Sidewalk Blues," and "Grandpa's Spells" are carefully etched miniatures, three-minute masterpieces.

But there are so many more, too, just from the 1920s alone—the recordings of Oscar "Papa" Celestin's Tuxedo Orchestra, and the Halfway House Orchestra, the New

Orleans Owls, Sam Morgan's Jazz Band (especially "Down by the Riverside" and "Short-Dress Gal"), the Jones & Collins Astoria Hot Eight doing "Damp Weather," "To-Wa-Bac-A-Wa" by Louis Dumaine's Jazzola Eight, Johnny Miller's New Orleans Frolickers, Monk Hazel's Bienville Roof Orchestra, A. J. Piron's Society Orchestra. . . . Each is in a sense a fragment of the whole picture, yet at the same time each of those three-minute recordings summons the entirety of that world, each one *is* a whole world in itself, a miniature society of contrasting musical personalities all pulling against each other and yet pulling together at the same time. What kind of place could have produced such a vision of the world, such elation and such lyricism mixed together, such individuality in the service of a communal effect?

And those are just the ones actually recorded in New Orleans; there were countless other musicians who, like Oliver and Morton (who performed and recorded in Chicago and Indiana) made up a kind of unprecedented musical diaspora. The 1926–28 recordings by Louis Armstrong's Hot Five and Hot Seven pointed the way to a style oriented more toward virtuoso soloing on recordings like "Potato Head Blues" and "Wild Man Blues" and "Cornet Chop Suey" and "West End Blues," one of the perfect jazz records, with its opening cadenza of such power and imagination and balance. Not to mention Johnny Dodds's "Perdido Street Blues," and "Cake Walking Babies from Home" by Clarence Williams' Blue Five, with the amazing jousting match between Louis Armstrong and soprano saxophonist Sidney Bechet, and countless others.

If New Orleans music were just jazz and no more it would still loom larger than any other art produced by Americans in the twentieth century. Even if one leaves aside the fact of so many great musicians, singers and entertainers from the Crescent City—Mahalia Jackson, Louis Prima, the Boswell Sisters—as an accident, the extraordinary musical culture of the late forties and fifties and beyond that produced rhythm and blues and rock and roll was no accident.

Ray Charles and Little Richard both made their best early recordings in New Orleans, accompanied by New Orleans musicians. On Ray Charles's "Mess Around," in fact, you can hear Ray play a piano figure that Jelly Roll Morton played years before on his "New Orleans Blues." Fats Domino, of course, was one of the archetypal rock-and-rollers, and all of his recordings (most of which were arranged and orchestrated by the Crescent City's Dave Bartholomew) are suffused with the New Orleans spirit.

But probably no one had a more profound influence than pianist and singer Henry Roeland Byrd, also known as Professor Longhair, a pianist who exported the Spanish tinge spoken of by Jelly Roll Morton, a kind of left-hand rhumba beat, and placed boogie-woogie and blues figures on top of it in the right hand. His songs, like "Tipitina" and "Go to the Mardi Gras," are perennial classics, and all you have to do is hear a few notes to know who you are listening to. He can be seen in action in Les Blank's great New Orleans documentary film *Always for Pleasure*, and at greater length alongside fellow Crescent City pianists Allen Toussaint and Tuts Washington in Stevenson Palfi's documentary *Piano Players Rarely Ever Play Together.*

But how could you leave out Percy Mayfield, Lloyd Price, James Booker, Ernie "Mother-In-Law" K-Doe, Lee Dorsey, Huey "Piano" Smith and the Clowns, the Meters and the Neville Brothers and Dr. John. . . . And so many more unknown outside of New Orleans except by dyed-in-the-wool music freaks, people like Smiley Lewis and Big Boy Myles and Eddie Bo and Sugar Boy Crawford, who did the original version of "Iko-Iko" (he called it "Jock-a-Mo"), later made famous by another New Orleans group, the Dixie Cups. And then there's the blind singer-guitarist Snooks Eaglin, a one-man encyclopedia of New Orleans music who may still be seen in action at clubs and bars and the annual Jazz and Heritage Festival.

At a friend's New York City loft in the late seventies, hanging out and playing ping-pong, I heard a sound coming out of his speakers that I didn't recognize. Often background music stays in its place, providing a sort of carrier frequency on top of which conversation and other activity rides. But something about this music was not immediately identifiable and classifiable, and it was reaching up through the surface of everything else that was going on as if to say, "Get out of the way—coming through."

The LP, when my friend located the cover for me, was like nothing else I'd ever seen, either. A line of men—black, on close inspection—were dressed in brightly colored costumes, one blue, one yellow, one pink, consisting of feathers and, on even closer inspection, small patches with colored pictures on them that turned out to have been composed of tiny colored beads sewn onto canvas panels, mosaic-style, to make images of eagles, Indians, battle scenes. The bright plumes made each man about twice as large as he was in actuality, feathers shooting up in an aurora over each head and fanning out in wings to the side, and they had long black braids hanging down on either side of their head. Under their names were designations like Flag Boy, Spy Boy, Big Chief. . . . They were called the "Wild Tchoupitoulas."

Over a powerful rhythm and blues background—played by the great funk band the Meters—the Indians chanted their songs, led most of the time by a grainy-voiced singer named Big Chief Jolly. *Indians*, he sang, in what sounded like good natured, cocky challenge, as much for his gang as for the listeners, *here dey come. Meet de boys on de battlefront*—the songs were all about boasts of prowess, how good his gang was, and what they would do to other gangs when they ran into them, the mayhem they would inflict, but the rhythm, the buoyancy of the music that carried these elegant rhymed boasts, was about dancing, not fighting. It was amazing.

It turned out that this group of men was only one of at least a dozen such groups in New Orleans, and that most of them don't make records, but make similar out-

fits every year in which they parade on Mardi Gras
singing songs like those on the record. They have names
like the Wild Magnolias (they had made a record, too, it
turned out), and the Yellow Pocahontas and the Creole
Osceolas and the White Eagles and the Ninth Ward
Hunters and the Creole Wild West. The members of the
gangs are mainly working-class African American men
who spend months before Mardi Gras every year putting
together their costumes, which they call "suits." Nobody
really knows the genesis of the Indians, although the oldest gang, the Creole Wild West, dates its founding to back
in the late 1800s. Some say interest was stirred up by Buf-
falo Bill's traveling Wild West Show; others claim that a
bond was forged between escaped slaves and local Indians
who sheltered them and gave them sanctuary. Nobody
knows for sure, just as guesses as to the etymology of the
Mardi Gras Indians' characteristic patois are notoriously
unreliable.

On Mardi Gras morning they assemble, going from
member's house to member's house, or sometimes meeting at an assigned place, and they roam through the streets
of the city, directed by the Big Chief and preceded by the
Spy Boy, whose job it is to initiate contact with other
gangs whose paths cross theirs. Once that happens, a large

crowd usually forms as the two Big Chiefs address one another, approaching down a corridor formed by dozens or
more people watching closely, shouting encouragement,
and listening to the intricate, rhymed boasts with which
the Chiefs test one another's presence of mind and lin-
guistic skill. They will usually brag about how "pretty"
their own suits are, showing off in stylized and very pre-
cise gestures, each of which, like the patois in which they
deliver their boasts, has a hermetic meaning understood
only by the Indians themselves.

Indians pride themselves on making a new suit, from
scratch, every year, in time for Mardi Gras. They decide on
a main color, then order feathers and plumes, and canvas
patches on which pictures and designs will be sketched
out, then beads and thread and needles to sew the beads to
the canvas patches, bringing the designs alive in phenome-
nal color and detail. Those patches are then sewed into the
entire suit to make an integrated effect that is stunning and
awe-inspiring no matter how many times you have seen it.
They parade, and have always paraded, through the streets
not only on Mardi Gras but on St. Joseph's Night, March
19, and, more recently, on what is called Super Sunday, the
Sunday nearest St. Joseph's Night, when all the Indians in
the city assemble together—uptown gangs in Shakespeare

Park, on Washington and LaSalle, and downtown gangs on Bayou St. John by the Orleans Avenue bridge. The uptown Indians concentrate on sewing representational scenes in their intricate beaded patches. Downtown Indians substitute elaborate 3-D geometrical constructions, encrusted with jewel-like pieces of glass and pearls.

The Wild Tchoupitoulas had a band behind them, but most of the time the gangs would rove the streets accompanied only by tambourines and drums and even beer bottles—anything that would rap out the characteristic rhythm as the Big Chief lined out a call and the rest of the gang would answer as follows:

> An Ace, a trey, a deuce and a jack . . .
> > *Shoo fly, don't bother me . . .*
> I been to Angola but I made it back
> > *Shoo fly, don't bother me . . .*
> I walk through fire and I swim through mud
> > *Shoo fly, don't bother me . . .*
> Snatch the feather from an eagle, drink panther
> > blood
> > *Shoo fly, don't bother me . . .*

That Wild Tchoupitoulas album grabbed hold of my heart and would not let go and it hasn't let go to this day. Down amid all those compelling funky-butt rhythms, and all those calls from the chief and responses from the gang, all that good-natured boasting, and the relentlessness of the groove that they set on each track, the mixture of good humor with something dead-serious, I heard the essence of what I had loved for years in jazz music, blues, bluegrass, and in rock and roll, that mixture of opposite qualities—gravity and buoyancy, go-for-yourself spontaneity and absolute rhythmic precision, seriousness and irony—delivered over certain rhythmic patterns that lived at the center of everything important to me. I recognized that rhythmic stew, with its call and response patterns and its Latin-French-African-Caribbean inflected rhythms, as the roots not just of jazz but of rhythm and blues as well as funk. It only surprised me a little bit when, much later, I heard Jelly Roll Morton reminisce, in the Library of Congress recordings, about hearing and seeing Mardi Gras Indians when he was a boy in New Orleans, and even running with one of the gangs as a spy boy. That meant that the Indian gangs went back into the nineteenth century. He sang a song that he remembered them singing, in their characteristic patois.

Hu–tan–nay

*Two–way pock–a–way . . .*

Hu–tan–nay

*Two–way pock–a–way . . .*

The Wild Tchoupitoulas sing the same song on their record, with a few tiny changes; they call it "Hey Mama."

On one of my first Mardi Gras mornings after I had moved to New Orleans I lay sick in bed with fever, to the degree that even contemplating going to the kitchen for a glass of water seemed like a logistical impossibility. I didn't care that it was Mardi Gras, or about anything else. It was still early, when I heard a banging on my front door, then the buzzer, urgent. Swimming up to the surface through the glue of sleep and fever I swung my legs over the side of the bed and made my way, shivering, to the front door.

Outside, a neighbor I knew stood there with an amazed expression on her face, pointing toward the corner, and saying, simply, "Look."

I didn't have to look to know what she was pointing at, because I could hear the tambourines and the chanting, but when I did look I saw three Indians in full regalia, coming down Plum Street—one in light purple, one in bright green, and one in orange. I couldn't believe my eyes: Indians passing right by my house. I was sure they were from the Carrolton Hunters, a gang I'd heard of but not yet seen in my time in New Orleans. They were singing:

> Let's go get 'em
> > *Hey pocky-way . . .*
> Let's go get 'em
> > *Hey pocky-way . . .*

And like Popeye with a sudden infusion of spinach, or a pilgrim throwing away his crutches at Lourdes, all I could think was, "Goddamn right—let's go get 'em." I went and got dressed as quickly as I could and ran after them. They had gotten to Adams Street and hung a right, and down at the corner of Oak Street they were joined by a couple more Indians, and some neighborhood folks, and they kept going down Adams and I followed them to Freret Street and then downtown across Broadway and down Freret as it bisected the Tulane campus and I must have followed them for the better part of a mile, chanting and singing along on the refrains before I realized that any distance I traveled with them I would have to retrace, in reverse, by myself—and soon, too, because I was all-too-obviously feverish. Finally I let them go, off into the distance, in a blaze of brightly colored spiritual glory, and went quickly back home and climbed back into bed. It was one of the happiest mornings I can remember.

Throughout the year the Indians hold regular "practices," usually on Sunday nights and usually at neighborhood bars. The practices are where they hone their improvisatory skills chanting and beating out rhythm on percussion instruments, as well as performing the stylized gestures involved in their characteristic dances; they are where the arcane lore of the Indians is handed down to younger members by the older ones, and where all partake of the special spiritual bond generated by the complex of sounds and movement characteristic of them, and at the root of New Orleans culture.

The Indians, like everything else in New Orleans, are not always what they might seem on the surface. The grand, mysterious figure leading his gang on Mardi Gras day might be a welder at a shipyard eating lunch next to his coworkers on any other given day of the year. Nor is the assumption of the mask of the Indian in any way a guarantee of primitivism. Here is an example of what I mean:

Shortly after I moved to New Orleans I happened to meet Big Chief Donald Harrison, Senior. Chief Donald was the father of jazz saxophonist Donald Harrison, and a well-known figure in the city, Chief of the Guardians of the Flame gang. I remember seeing him at gatherings engaging in chanted verbal battle with other chiefs, but I no longer remember how we struck up our brief conversation. It was short but he recognized my interest—New Orleans is characterized above all by its generosity and its spirit of welcome—and invited me to attend an Indian practice the next Sunday night, to be held at the Treme Music Hall, a bar located in the historic black neighborhood that stretches from Rampart Street away from the river for blocks and blocks, the oldest continually occupied African American neighborhood in the United States.

I showed up that Sunday not at all sure what to expect, but imagining it would involve a lot of percussion and singing. I was new to the city, and I had cruised around at daytime in all kinds of areas, but this was the first time I had gone alone, at night, into the heart of a black neighborhood in the Crescent City. In my New York days I had done it in Harlem, but this was still unfamiliar territory to me, and one with a less cosmopolitan surface than New York's Harlem. I wasn't afraid, but I was alert. I would go in and out of these neighborhoods plenty in the years that followed, and have learned that there were reasons to feel more comfortable than I did, as well as reasons to be less comfortable, but they were all under the surface, often inscrutable. It was an elaborate, coded language of behavior, one you had to learn.

Nothing in New Orleans starts on time, and this practice was no exception. I stood at the bar alone for at least half an hour, listening to the jukebox in the nearly empty room, waiting for Big Chief Donald. People began to filter in slowly, no way to tell whether they were Indians or not. Nobody made me feel uncomfortable or out of place, and in fact nobody seemed to notice me at all, although I am sure they did. Eventually a thin figure in a stingy-brim porkpie hat approached me through the gloomy half-light, and I recognized him as Chief Donald. The last time I had seen him he was decked out in powder blue plumes and feathers, engaged in a verbal duel with some other chief whose identity I can't remember— it might have been Larry Bannock of the Golden Star Hunters. In any case here he was, in mufti.

I don't remember what he drank or what I drank; I just remember chatting with him for a while about this and that. When he asked me what kind of work I did, I told him that I wrote books, and magazine articles. He asked me what kind, and I told him that I wrote fiction and nonfiction, a lot about music. I asked him if he liked to read and he told me he did; when I asked him what he liked to read he said, "Mainly philosophy, and some fiction. I have an extensive library of books on philosophy and African American history as well."

By that time in my life I had had enough experience with a wide range of American culture not to be surprised to come across things that weren't what they seemed on the surface, yet this surprised me. I thought I knew what and who the Mardi Gras Indians were; despite everything I knew, or thought I knew, about the way things worked in this culture, I was surprised to hear this man—whom I had seen dressed in elaborate Indian regalia, plumes and feathers sprouting, chanting African-based rhythms over tambourine background—say that he read philosophy. To my shame, I had a moment of skepticism that lay beneath my next question, which was, "Which philosophers do you like to read?"

"Lately," he said, "mainly Bertrand Russell. But I love Nietzsche too."

★   ★   ★

It is an old American situation, of course—anyone interested in an extended essay on the subject should read Ralph Ellison's "The Little Man at Chehaw Station," in his collection *Going to the Territory,* or Constance Rourke's *American Humor,* both extended meditations on the masks not just that we put on *for* others but that we put *on* others, the surprises that lurk so often around the corners of someone's seemingly straightforward identity. It is a lesson that one has to learn continually in New Orleans. Things are always more complex than they seem. This is true of any city, but in New Orleans it has its special flavors, as does everything in the Crescent City. I probably could have learned it elsewhere, but I would have learned it more slowly, and it wouldn't have been as much fun.

# 4.

Every year, since 1970, the New Orleans Jazz and Heritage Festival—Jazz Fest—has come to the Crescent City as spring comes to the rest of the country. For two weekends, the last in April and the first in May, New Orleans's racetrack, better known as the fairgrounds, becomes a small city in itself. For eight hours a day, Friday, Saturday, and Sunday (with the Thursday between the weekends thrown in for good measure), eight or nine stages, strategically placed around the grounds, serve up jazz, gospel, cajun, zydeco, New Orleans rhythm and blues, a little country, some flat-out rock, straight blues, rockabilly, and a sampling of Caribbean, Haitian, Latino and African musics. Tens of thousands of people, from New Orleans and around the world, hear this music each day.

Throughout the sprawling racetrack infield, rows of

wooden booths wind and curve, offering an array of
Louisiana food prepared by local chefs, one or two special
dishes to each booth. Also clustered in the infield are
many other booths, where local artisans demonstrate traditional crafts like furniture making, instrument making,
various old-time ways of cooking and weaving; clothing,
hats, and crafts of almost any description are available for
sale as well. There are also a book tent and a tent where
you can buy compact discs and cassettes of the artists ap-
pearing at the Fest. Periodically, amid the crowds of people milling around through all this, the sound of a brass
band flares up behind you and a marching band ap-
proaches in full cry, accompanied by one of the city's
many marching clubs decked out in full regalia, matching
suits and hats, bright and beribboned sashes across their
torso, waving brightly colored matching feathered fans
and cutting steps that would humble any dancer, and
which will be found nowhere but in New Orleans.

Before I lived in New Orleans, Jazz Fest was the gravita-
tional center of my year. I lived through the long, gray
New York winter, or the howling, wild Iowa winter,
which lasted until the middle of April, and Jazz Fest

would loom like a rescue ship on the horizon. If it was a year when I would be lucky enough to attend both weekends and stay the week in between, my only thought was Please don't let a car hit me between now and the end of April.

New Orleans, in fact, is filled with people who came for Jazz Fest and never left. Or who went home and quit their job and came back. I think Jazz Fest teaches them what to love about the city, and how to love it. It is a kind of distillation of the mythology of the city.

Jazz Fest constantly underlines the relationship between the music of New Orleans (and Louisiana) and the culture as a whole. The food, the parades, the crafts, are all part of a larger fabric, as they are in the city itself. You won't find posters advertising individual artists' appearances at the fairgrounds. Music, the logic seems to run, is bigger than any individual's music. And, furthermore, culture is bigger than music. Jazz Fest brings this notion into focus, gives it life, better than any other event I know of.

If you are ambitious enough to get yourself up toward Bayou St. John in the mid-morning of a Jazz Fest day, you can find a parking space not too far from the Fairgrounds and walk through the beautiful oak-lined streets with their crumbling sidewalks and big shipwrecked houses, across Esplanade Avenue, and maybe past Liuzza's bar, where they're already doing a brisk business in beer that will have to be consumed before its drinkers hit the gates. Thousands of people converge via the narrow streets toward one of two entrances. You cross a parking lot area, top a slight rise, and before you lies the expanse of the Fairgrounds—the stages, the food booths, all of it—with a light haze over it from the dust of the track which never seems to settle completely.

Before you arrive, you have probably circled acts you want to see on the schedule that you cut out of the newspaper and placed, folded, in your back pocket, next to the kerchief that you'll wrap around your head as the day gets hotter. At the Gospel Tent, the Word is already being pumped out at top volume over throbbing organ riffs. Across the infield and through the African-village style stalls, past the blacksmith who is already set up in his own little corral demonstrating his trade, a Cajun band is playing at the Fais Do-do Stage, and you can grab a dance with one of the hundred or so people who are already there.

Later in the day you can see the big national acts, of course—Willie Nelson, Bob Dylan, Bela Fleck, Emmylou Harris, Dave Matthews, Jimmy Buffett, Aretha Franklin.

But the real reason to come to the Fairgrounds, especially for those who don't live in New Orleans, is not to see the big famous acts, but to hear the local heroes, like Snooks Eaglin, who is one of the greatest musical treasures in the United States. Sitting in a chair on a stage in the hot sun wearing aviator shades over his eyes, which have been blind since childhood, talking back and forth with the audience, shouting with pleasure, goading the other musicians with him, sometimes picking the guitar up and playing it behind his head, jumping from "Lipstick Traces" to "Malaguena" to the old jazz tune "High Society" to some obscure New Orleans rhythm and blues tune. . . .

There are other local treasures, of course, too many to count, some of them all but unknown outside of town. Like Deacon John, for example. For upward of forty years, he and his band have played the house parties and the little clubs, the high school proms and the Tulane dances, serving up the good-time music. Deacon John and the Ivories. You will probably catch him in the mid-afternoon, and probably at one of the smaller stages. His band will be onstage without him as he is introduced; they kick off a shuffle blues and play at least a full chorus with no Deacon John in evidence anywhere. Then, at the top of the second chorus, a heavy, Elmore James–style slide guitar rides in on top of the band, still no Deacon John visible, and then, to the side of the stage, the door to one of the dressing room trailers opens, and there's Deacon John himself, taking his time, grinning broadly, playing his guitar, which is picked up with a remote mike, walking step by wooden step down from the trailer and making his way to the stage along the police barricades, where the fans gather and cheer—you could reach out and touch him—slowly he makes his way to the stage, and everybody is smiling, and when he hits the mike he hollers,

*I'm getting up early in the morning; I believe I'll dust my broom. . . .*

. . . and he's no genius, no originator, but what he does he does great, and he's been doing it for forty years, and he goes for broke every time, jumping down off the stage, sitting on the edge of the stage, a showman in the old Guitar Slim mold. . . . the point being to revive the good times, make them rock once again, for one more night, one more afternoon. The music is bigger than he is, and he knows it; he is there in the service of the good times, not the other way around.

Sooner or later, you will get very hungry. This is not a problem at Jazz Fest. The only problem is pacing yourself so that you can eat as much of what you want as possible. You burn a lot of it off walking around and dancing in the hot sun. The food is prepared by people who compete to sell the one or two dishes that any given booth is allowed to sell. Only one booth may sell fried chicken, only one may sell crawfish etouffee, etc. There are no national chain restaurants represented at the Fairgrounds, only local virtuosos.

Everyone has their favorite food at Jazz Fest, and people are partisan about the food they like. For instance, the *cochon de lait* (suckling pig) po' boy, a sandwich served on French bread. The *cochon de lait* is undeniably delicious, and I too, for a while, was a devotee. But then I discovered the fried turkey po' boy. Fried turkey is a delicacy immensely popular in Louisiana for special occasions; it bears no relation to fried chicken, as there is no batter or bread crumbs. The entire turkey is seasoned and cooked in a deep tub of boiling oil. They put the slices on some French bread with a little mayonnaise and salt, and they used to lay some turkey skin in there with it, as well, which was what made it special. At some point they stopped putting in the skin, perhaps because all their cus-

tomers were dying from heart attacks, and I switched back
to *cochon de lait.*

There are some foods upon which everyone agrees.
There is the Crawfish Monica booth, for example, which
always has long lines; their signature dish is *fusilli* macaroni
in a delicious cream sauce with big crawfish tails in it. It's
good early-in-the-day food, with plenty of carbohydrates
for energy and endurance, and it's easier on the stomach
than some of the things you can buy. Also extremely popular are the crawfish sacks, little edible dough sacks tied
up with a green chive and deep fried, also served with
fried green tomatoes. And there are the omnipresent
snowball booths, always welcome on a hot day. And you
eat all this food standing out in the sun, talking to friendly
strangers about what they've seen and hope to see during
the day.

Jazz Fest resembles Mardi Gras in at least one way,
which is that many people use it as an occasion to adopt
alternative identities. Many come to have a good time of
a type that they may not wish to have posted to their Permanent Record. I learned this the first time I went to
Jazz Fest, watching the Creole Wild West Mardi Gras Indians. The stage was pulsating, with feathers of bright
blue, red, pink, sky blue, fire engine yellow, canary red, as

tambourines and other rhythm instruments beat out a rhythm.

Next to me, right up in front, I noticed a guy a little older than I was at the time, about forty maybe, although it was hard to tell. He was wearing sunglasses, a coolie-style bamboo hat festooned with buttons advertising Bob Marley, cannabis sativa, and Professor Longhair; from beneath the hat, covering his neck, a miniature Jamaican flag hung down French foreign legion style. His electric-green and fuchsia Hawaiian shirt hung open over a black T-shirt with a picture of the New Orleans pianist James Booker on it, and as he swayed in time to the Indians' chants he smoked a thin brown Nat Sherman cigarillo. His bony white legs stuck out from underneath his shorts. I figured he was some kind of band roadie or permanent Deadhead, a part-time house painter and beer connoisseur. We started talking, and after we watched the Indians together for a while, he told me to call him later in the week. He reached into his back pocket, pulled out his wallet and flipped me a business card; he was the chief cardiologist at the biggest hospital in Baton Rouge (actual department and hospital changed to protect the innocent).

★　★　★

The important thing about Jazz Fest, and the secret of its alchemy, is that the music doesn't exist in a vacuum; it is carefully set into its cultural context at the fairgrounds and, by extension, in the city. There is music going constantly at all the city's clubs, and the week between the Jazz Fest weekends is one of the busiest weeks of the year for the clubs in New Orleans. Sitting out on the grass outside Tipitina's watching the freight trains roll by on the levee at two in the morning, drinking a beer and listening to the music drifting out of the club, is an integral part of the whole experience. It is the spirit of New Orleans itself, finally, that is the message of Jazz Fest.

Back when I first started coming to Jazz Fest I'd always rent a bike and ride all over town, anywhere, any time of the day or night. After the concerts the clubs are always hopping, then and now, and one of the best places to go is the Maple Leaf Bar, way uptown. On my first visit I went there to hear Rockin' Dopsie (senior), with his fine zydeco band that he had inherited more or less wholesale from the late, great Clifton Chenier. It was my first time dancing to zydeco; of course I didn't know how to dance to it, and it was hot, and I remember the exact moment when I felt my glasses slide off my face, and fall, and I saw them break on the floor. I examined them closely—the temple piece had snapped right where it at-tached to the front of the glasses—then I put them in my pocket and resumed dancing.

After the band was finished, way deep in the morn-ing, I got on my rent-a-bike and headed off for the long ride from Oak Street all the way back down to the lower Garden District guest house where I was sleeping on a cot in the kitchen. I headed down Carrolton Avenue, the glasses held provisionally on my face by only one temple piece. The other was in my pocket. I am useless without my glasses, and this was a temporary situation, at best.

When I got to the bend in the river, where Car-rolton makes a hard turn to the left and becomes St. Charles Avenue, there were two gas stations, one of which was open all night, and I decided to see if they had any glue. I rode the bike up to the little plexiglas window, where a tired-looking young black woman sat reading a book. Sculpted, layered hair, and impressively long, deco-rated fingernails. It had to be three in the morning, at least. She looked up at me, expressionlessly, her eyes watching for the clues of who I was and what I wanted. I leaned down to the little drawer that could be slid back and forth for change.

"Do you have Krazy Glue?"

She frowned at me, unsure just what I was saying.

"Do you sell Krazy Glue?" I repeated. "Or any kind of glue? My glasses," and here I removed my glasses, demonstrating the brokenness of them, "broke. I was dancing at the Maple Leaf . . ."

She looked at my glasses, and then she smiled, understanding now what the problem was. With a regretful smile she looked at me and shook her head. No glue.

I smiled back at her; it was a long shot anyway. I stood there another moment or two, looking at my glasses. As I was about to turn away, she said over her little microphone, "Let me see them, darling."

She pushed out the steel change drawer, and I set the glasses and the temple piece in the drawer, and she drew it in toward her. She rummaged around in her purse. After a moment she found what she was looking for, a tiny vial; she unscrewed the cap and, looking intently at the break spot, examining it first, applied the nib of the little vial to it, then took the temple piece, fit it right in to where it was broken, and held it there, steadily, looking at it, with the beginning of a pleased, self-congratulatory smile. After about ten seconds she removed her hand from the temple piece, which remained in position, sticking up in the air; she blew on the joint, then set the glasses into the tray again, along with the vial.

I pulled out the glasses, which were now fine, put them on; they fit fine. Then I looked at the vial; it was fingernail-repair glue. I looked at her questioningly and she waved me off. "I can get more," she said. "I have more at home. Take it." That may have been the moment when I really fell in love with New Orleans.

And maybe late in the day you will finally work your way around to one of the big stages at either end of the Fairgrounds' ellipse and get in as close as possible and hear the Fat Man, Fats Domino himself. Everybody has been waiting for him; he doesn't perform that often anymore. A drive by his unmistakable house in the Ninth Ward is, or was, an essential stop on any Music Tour of the Crescent City (it flooded to the roof during Hurricane Katrina). Fats stayed in New Orleans, unlike many of the more successful musicians who leave to be closer to the Action, and everyone in New Orleans loves Fats Domino. When you get to the big stage his band is already assembled—there is Herb Hardesty himself, on tenor, a lot of the old timers, and finally the announcement comes and the band starts playing and Fats himself comes out from backstage and sits at the big black grand piano, one more time, the lord of the good times, as big as ever, the ring on his right hand visible from a half mile away, that bob of the head as he delivers the old, well-known lyrics about finding his thrill on Blueberry Hill, or asking Josephine if she remembers him like he remembers her, or telling us why they call him, they call him, the Fat Man. His voice is terrific, that old Creole accent, and he performs for ninety minutes at least, and he looks like he is having as much fun as anyone, just to be out there, doing it again; he plays long piano solos, and there's room for horn solos, and Fats smiles at the band as he plays, talks to them, hollers at them; everybody on stage is smiling, it's a party, and the subtext, as it always is in New Orleans, is that we're all still alive and we might not be tomorrow.

At the end of the set, after "I'm in Love Again," and "Ain't It a Shame," and "Blue Monday," and all the rest of it, Fats Domino stands up and, in time to the music—is it "Sentimental Journey"?—starts pushing the gigantic grand piano across the stage with his pelvis, playing it all the while—forget Jerry Lee Lewis, great as he is, kicking his stool over; Fats is PUSHING the damn piano, ham-

mering out those chords in triplets, and the band is riff-
ing, and people in the audience are climbing on each others' shoulders and screaming with happiness as the sun
slides down the sky toward another evening, and everybody who is there will remember it for the rest of their
lives.


It was the end of the day, the last day, Sunday, of my second Jazz Fest. I guess Dr. John had just gotten through at
the big stage closest to Gentilly Boulevard, a little after
seven o'clock, and the sun was down but it was still light
enough to make your way along and hazy and orange in
the sky and people were draining toward the exits in
slow-moving swarms, moving slowly because they knew it
was the end, for that year, and my glasses had come apart
yet again. Somehow one of the little screws that held the
left temple piece onto the front had come disengaged and
fallen into the ground, and I found myself crouched in the
dying light, scrabbling blindly around on the ground looking for it, with the people moving around me, feeling like
an abandoned child during the retreat from Stalingrad.

"Hey, you all right?"

I looked up; above me stood two men and a woman,

looking down at me with no special expression of concern, but they had stopped.

"Yeah," I said. "I lost a screw out of my glasses, though, and I guess it's gone . . ."

"Whut'd he say?"

"He said he's lookin for a screw . . ." Laughter.

"What's it for?"

"My glasses," I said. "It'll be okay," I said, tousling the weedy, trampled grass a little more with my fingers, searching.

"Where you from?"

"New York City," I said.

"New York?" they said, almost in chorus. "Oh, dude. You came all the way down here to come to Jazz Fest?"

"Yeah," I said. The screw search was pretty much turning out hopeless. "Where are you from?"

"Poplarville."

"Where?"

"Poplarville, Mississippi. It's just up across the state line."

"Here," I heard the woman's voice saying.

I looked up; she was holding something out to me. I stood up, and it was a tiny screw. "Where'd you find this?" I asked.

"I took it out of my sunglasses," she said. She was holding her disassembled sunglasses in one hand. "Don't worry," she said. "They're cheap ones. Try it see if it fits."

It fit, or well enough, at least, to hold me until I got back to New York. "Hey," I said. "Hey, listen . . . thanks . . ."

They were already starting to head away. "That's all right," one of the guys said. "Yeah," the other said. "Tell 'em up in New York the folks in Poplarville are okay, nice people. Some of us even got teeth . . ." and they moved off, laughter spraying up and out of their little group like confetti.

And then, as all things must, it passes; Jazz Fest is over for another year. The stages are all taken down, and the garbage picked up, and the food booths disassembled, and the sound systems stashed away in innumerable cases. The flags and streamers are hauled down, and the only sound at the Fairgrounds is what drifts in from the traffic on Gentilly Boulevard. A kind of sadness, a flatness, descends on New Orleans. The circus, after all, has left town.

But then, not too long afterward—maybe a week and a half, maybe two—you notice an ad in the paper. Snooks Eaglin is going to be at Mid-City Lanes on Saturday night. It seems to be about time for a plate of trout at Uglesich's, or maybe a steak at Charlie's. Life does go on, as even the funerals here remind us. They say nothing lasts forever, but how, one might ask, do they know?

# 5.

Sooner or later, New Orleans will test any love you bring to it. At first, for many, it is a spangled, dancing place, the City that Care Forgot, arm in arm down midnight streets, toasting life, Spanish moss and delicious food, gorgeous architecture, sensuality and more sensuality, a willingness to go where the day leads you. If you are a visitor with money to spend, you might not notice the person clearing away your dishes, or washing them in the restaurant kitchen, or cleaning your room while you are out at Galatoire's having lunch.

If you come to town and see a parade passing with hundreds of celebrants smiling and dancing behind it, holding up beer cans, hugging one another in greeting, or perhaps hanging back a little around the edges, looking for a chance, it is easy to miss the fact that that great multifarious unity of the parade, with all that it represents, consists of many individual, complex lives, people who can neither read nor write alongside people who read Shakespeare, people who have never been outside of New Orleans and people whose sons and daughters go to college because of sacrifices they made that are hard even for a middle-class person to imagine. Most of them have to struggle just to cover the basics for themselves and their families.

New Orleans is a city of elegance, beauty, refinement, and grace. It is also a city of violence, poor education, and extreme poverty of a type that you can't imagine if you haven't actually seen it. Even in its most desperate precincts it is a city of deep and powerful humanity, of endurance, resilience, humor and affirmation in the face of adversity. Yet it may be worth stating what should be obvious: the good times, in New Orleans as elsewhere, ride on the ill-paid efforts of people who did not get certain breaks.

There is no way to avoid this fact if you are going to discuss New Orleans honestly; it is part of what makes the city what it is, and part of why all the beauty—human and physical—of the city represents such a triumph of humanity. In the black gospel tradition, which is so central to New Orleans culture, there is a saying: "No cross, no crown." If you don't accept the burden of your humanity and your finiteness and your suffering and, perhaps more important, that of the people around you, you will never reach the ennobling reward that the word Heaven represents to a believer. You can't have a triumph without triumphing over something—whether from outside or from within yourself. No cross, no crown.

Louisiana in general has one of the weakest economies in the nation, and New Orleans, in particular, is a place of great contrast between its wealthiest citizens and its poorest citizens. In many other places, the well-off and the poor are separated geographically and do not have much day-to-day personal contact. In New Orleans you can walk out the front door, if it has a door, of a house that is falling down, in a neighborhood full of such houses, and walk five blocks and stand in front of mansions that people from around the world save their money and spend their leisure time to travel and see. This proximity of the poorest citizens to the wealthiest and most entitled ones has many ramifications, not all of them chartable on any sociologist's map.

To some extent, the problems in New Orleans resemble those found in parts of any major American urban area, exacerbated by the infiltration of drug use and a culture of thuggishness and rapacity often encouraged by the media. Shootings are a regular feature of life—usually in the projects or poor neighborhoods, but not always. Hardly a month goes by without a report of a toddler shot to death, usually by accident; if you take the *Times-Picayune* and read it over eggs benedict and fresh-squeezed orange juice, you will doubtless shake your head at the photo accompanying the article, usually a smiling studio portrait of some hopeful three-year-old face.

If you live somewhere closer to the action, you may not need the photo to remember that girl or boy, and maybe you are even the one who, sobbing, loaned the photo to the solicitous person from the newspaper. Maybe your half-brother's three kids are there behind you in the living room, along with his new girlfriend, who is sitting on a brand-new couch that is the only piece of furniture in the bare room aside from a folding chair on a bare floor against a dirty wall under a single light bulb on the ceiling. Maybe there is a television, too; if it's someone's mama's house maybe it's an old one and the knobs don't work which is why there's a pair of pliers on the floor next to the set; if it's someone's sister's house, or cousin's, maybe you don't worry about the controls because you have a remote, which your half-brother's new girlfriend just smacked her youngest son's face, hard, for touching.

Some poor folks' houses have books and most don't. Some are owned or rented by people who work and some by people who don't work. Few of them are classic nuclear-family arrangements; almost always they contain extended families that struggle to manage despite members being in prison, or mothers who had to travel to California for work, leaving two children with a sister-in-law and her boyfriend and their three kids. Maybe the sister-in-law and her boyfriend find time to read to the kids in the evening. Probably they don't. The majority of them work very hard at jobs that nobody wants, on shifts nobody wants, taking buses that connect to other buses to get there, an hour and a half each way, coming in standing all the way from East New Orleans, or out from the Lower Nine all the way to the nice, or not-so-nice, white lady's house in Old Metairie. Maybe they are worried about their brother who is at Angola, or their mother who has diabetes and may have to have her leg amputated and then she'll be in a wheelchair and how are they going to get her in and out of the house and how will she stay clean and who is going to take care of Toya's three children when she's working at the parking lot from eight P.M. to six A.M.? And then they killed Javon, they know exactly who did it, it wasn't that they were trying to kill a three-year-old, he just got in the way, and that poor boy lay there on the sidewalk and the police took forty-five minutes to get there and then they start treating the boy's family members like they're the criminals.

If you are black in New Orleans you are almost never too far or too insulated from those facts, even if you are not poor. Even if you have a good union job at the post office or at Avondale or the Sewerage and Water Board, or you drive a bus, or you are a nurse, you or some close family member will likely be touched personally by violence. Even after you spend all those hours on buses, or maybe even in your Toyota, driving to work, and maybe save up to buy some little birthday present for one of the kids at Walgreen's, or a even book for your niece or son at Barnes & Noble, and you are lucky enough to have a stable family and a nice house with new carpeting (which you are nervous about anybody spilling anything on), white people will often treat you as if you are invisible, or a joke, or a borderline criminal. Or they will disrespect your mother in front of you, or treat you, a grown man who has raised five children, like a child. They will expect you to be cheerful when you wait on them, to give them a little jive to make them feel as if everything's okay, or if you are driving them in from the airport in one of the shuttle vans that you drive ten hours a day to help support your sister's kids they will expect you to give them good tips on what restaurants to go to, or to tell them how nice the day is and to warn them about the "bad" areas, and then to make some kind of joke at your own expense.

It is easy to point to the violence and poverty and ignorance and illiteracy that plague large tracts of the New Orleans community, as the Problem That Needs To Be Fixed. But they don't exist in a vacuum. New Orleans suffers from a level of official corruption and ineptitude and mismanagement that is as astonishing as the poverty. The problems come, as they always do, from a tangled web of other problems.

The public schools in New Orleans are some of the worst in the nation. Ceilings are falling in, lights burn out and are never replaced, books—when there are books—are destroyed by leaks, or by vandalism from youngsters who never had anybody to teach them how to control their impulses or their anger. It is hard to learn anything in a classroom where half the lights are out and the teacher and the administration have all they can do just to maintain a semblance of order. Partly this has to do with the fact that many white, well-off citizens with school-age kids moved out of Orleans Parish, or put their children in private schools, when the city's schools were ordered to be integrated in 1960. Much of the city's tax base collapsed right there.

Then there is the police force. Police departments are always extraordinarily complex and highly charged social ecosystems, but the NOPD is in a league of its own. My partner, Mary, is a civil rights lawyer who spends much of her time representing citizens who have been messed over in one way or another by the police. So I have seen some aspects of the interaction between cops and the communities more closely than I might have otherwise, and more than I would have liked.

It needs to be said that most New Orleans cops are

hardworking, decent men and women, black and white, who take their jobs and responsibilities seriously, amid many difficulties, not the least of which is a culture of bad behavior among some of their brother and sister officers. A significant percentage of those brother and sister officers participate in a kind of cowboy culture; they act as entrepreneurs, independent franchises, freelance badasses whose own antisocial impulses rival those of the thugs they are supposed to be controlling. The famous case of Len Davis, an officer who put out a murder contract on a woman who had filed brutality charges against him, is just one of the most sensational examples of a subculture of inexcusable brutality and creepiness. Many women have had the experience of being stopped by an officer to find that they had committed no definable offense except looking attractive to a bored cop in a patrol car. During Hurricane Katrina the department fell apart completely; 15 percent of the department deserted, left their posts completely; some estimates are higher than that. And a number were, themselves, seen looting.

The neighborhoods of New Orleans aren't just names on a map; they are organisms within a larger organism, with ongoing lives of their own. In parts of New Orleans there are still people—or there were, until Katrina—who have rarely been out of their neighborhood in their lives. The pace of change has been very slow in New Orleans, and many of these neighborhoods have maintained much of their character over the last century. Partly this is because the city is economically depressed. There just isn't much incentive to cannibalize areas in a constant search for profit, as there is in, say, New York City, where some areas become unrecognizable every ten years or so.

There are some notable exceptions to this, and they tend to occur at the extremes of the city's socio-economic spectrum. Much of the Central Business District, universally known as the CBD, with its office buildings, handful of skyscrapers, new hotels, parking ramps, Superdome and the rest of it, occupies land that was once home to some of the poorest and toughest people in the city; Louis Armstrong was born in this area, and some of the city's most notable honky-tonks were located there as well, including spots that played host to King Oliver, Jelly Roll Morton, and jazz's legendary progenitor cornetist, Buddy Bolden. All of that is gone now, except for one small part, a block stretching uptown on Rampart

Street from the corner of Perdido where Louis Armstrong used to run errands and a small theater featured black vaudeville and the corner saloon hosted Buddy Bolden more than once.

Periodically, alliances will form of snarky business-men and corrupt and semi-corrupt politicos, like a hurricane forming out in the Gulf of Mexico, or a pack of wild dogs, and move toward the heart of something beautiful with the intention of razing it, making a few bucks, and then moving on. Perhaps the most infamous example was the decision to run Interstate 10 directly through the heart of the city's historic African American section, the Treme. The section of Claiborne Avenue now in perpetual cement twilight, echoing with the tires of cars and trucks overhead, was once a broad boulevard where the Mardi Gras Indians would parade and social clubs would have picnics. It will tell you something about New Orleans to know that the Indians still parade there, and the social clubs and neighborhood groups still have picnics and parties there, in that gloomy concrete canyon that bisects a neighborhood that they refuse to let die.

They also tried to run a loop of the interstate along

the river, something like New York's West Side Highway, which would certainly have been a tasty treat for some consortium of contractors, but that one got stopped. It would have killed the French Quarter's charm, and one would have regarded that miracle of the Mississippi making its long curve from underneath the booming echoes that you now hear up at Claiborne. Needless to say, the people defending the Quarter had more money and more political clout than the people who lived on either side of Claiborne Avenue.

New Orleans has also experienced the twin 1990s phenomena of hyperventilated gentrification and the dry rot of drugs and thugs. In some areas, real estate prices nearly doubled in the three years before Hurricane Katrina. Neighborhoods began to change character. Lower Magazine Street, which was home to countless fantastic downscale antique shops and used furniture caverns and winos and funky flavor when I first visited, is becoming a long run of elegant shops and restaurants; it is undergoing that same process of petrification that the French Quarter did with the arrival of the Hard Rock Café and Planet Hollywood (now gone).

None of this gentrification ever takes hold quite

completely in New Orleans. There is a strong undertow of mistrust for it; people know on some level that these kinds of development don't really represent the spirit of the city the way they represent the spirit of more econocentric burgs, particularly in the North. The spasms of corruption, the fiefdoms of graft and profiteering and greed and power lust, raised to an art form in Louisiana government (see A.J. Liebling's great book *The Earl of Louisiana*), never get raised to the level of competence and professionalism exhibited by the real big-time *machers,* the Robert Moses types, or the Donald Trumps. People in Louisiana don't have ambitions on that scale, and they can't bring themselves to take their ambitions that seriously or make large claims for them.

And, at the other end of the economic spectrum, other neighborhoods have lost their character because of an active drug-and-gangster culture that has made the city a much more dangerous place. Some areas that had been poor as poor gets, yet still had an intact neighborhood culture, have been turned essentially into dukedoms and baronets controlled by drug dealers, featuring all the burnt-out houses, semi-automatic gunfire, and other elements that populate the movies and video games we all enjoy so much.

★  ★  ★

For some reason or complex of reasons, Louisiana politicians in general, and New Orleans politicians in particular, have turned the official corruption and patronage that
always come with government into an art form. Sometimes it is a crude folk art, sometimes a highly developed,
polished, and complex fine art, usually somewhere in between, but it is an art. I think it is difficult at this point for
Louisianians to fully trust any politician who isn't trying
to bilk them. They don't understand their motives otherwise. Often the worst and most fraudulent are the most
beloved, like the rogue lover whom everyone tells you to
dump but whom you just can't get out of your system.
Take former governor Edwin Edwards, for example, who
is one of the most charming men around, even in the Fort
Worth federal prison, where he is serving a ten-year sen-
tence after being convicted on seventeen counts of rack-
eteering, extortion, fraud, and conspiracy.

People love Edwards. When David Duke ran for
governor of the state in 1991, he stirred up an embarrass-
ing amount of support in Louisiana. To this day, in fact, in
some outlying parishes, you will still see fresh blue-and-
white Duke for Governor posters, usually placed twelve

or fifteen feet up on a telephone pole, out of reach of the many other Louisianians, white and black, who would otherwise tear them down as quickly as they were put up. The only person widely regarded as having a chance of beating Duke was former governor Edwards, for whom much of Duke's constituency also felt great affection. Everyone who hated what Duke stood for pooled their efforts behind Edwards's candidacy, even those who hated the corruption that Edwards stood for. Bumper stickers were printed up reading "Vote for the Crook—It's Important." Edwards was quoted as saying, "The only way I could lose this race is if I was caught in bed with a live boy or a dead girl." He won.

Still, his kind of corruption is responsible for the siphoning off of funds earmarked for all kinds of programs, the cynicism about government, the bypassing of trained and competent contractors in favor of political cronies, the smothering of genuine opportunity . . . in other words, it is a snake that strangles the core principles of democracy that America espouses. Edwards and his ilk remind me of Orson Welles's Harry Lime in *The Third Man*—the charming con man whose sinister dealings are enabled by the people who can't stay immune to his charm. It is hard to draw the line between forgivable ro-

guishness and profoundly corrosive abuse in a place like
Louisiana, partly because the rogue is usually a known
quantity. He can be trusted, in a sense, because people
know exactly how he can't be trusted. As Randy New-
man sang of Georgia governor Lester Maddox in his
seriocomic song "Rednecks": "He might be a fool, but
he's our fool." That mentality is one definition of provin-
cialism, and con men have taken advantage of it for mil-
lennia. Once, a few years back, I tried to buy a used car in
a New Orleans dealership. I tried one out in the lot; the
salesman sat in the passenger seat, smoking a cigarette. As
I turned left, the right front axle began making a clanking
sound.

"Well, okay," I said, "that takes care of this one."

"Now wait a minute," the salesman said. "We can
fix that. Wouldn't you rather buy a car where you knew
what's wrong instead of one where you can't tell?"


But official corruption and mendacity is only one part of
the story. The other part is what nobody wants to talk
about, and everyone can't stop talking about: racism. New
Orleans is in some ways one of the least racist places in

the country, if you measure by how much mixing actually goes on among black and white citizens. Many of the people who choose to live there, as opposed to those who happen to be born there, choose it in large part because of this fact, with all the complications it brings.

And yet it is still the South, and someone who comes from another region, as I did, can be blindsided by the ease and freedom with which people across the class spectrum express opinions that many hold elsewhere but have been trained not to actually express.

An example, perhaps the first time I found this out: I had come to New Orleans for the wedding of a friend whose wife had been born and grew up there. It was maybe my third or fourth visit to New Orleans and I knew my way around, more or less. I took the train down from New York and rented a bicycle, as I always did, and on my first day there I heard that the Zulu Social Aid and Pleasure Club was having their big anniversary parade. Of course this was not to be missed, and as the day was free from wedding responsibilities I lit out on my bike.

I spent the afternoon roving through the projects and the dilapidated streets, trying to find the parade, finding it, walking along with my bike, then riding some more. All of black New Orleans seemed to be celebrating, even blocks away from the parade proper. Smiling men in pickup trucks waved at me and held up bottles and glasses; little spin-off parades—tornados in the wake of the hurricane—passed, tossing out beads and souvenir cups and doubloons from Mardi Gras parades from three years before. One man in a car even passed me a fresh beer out the window of his car. I had the best time. Up on the neutral ground on Broad Street, on the block in front of the Zulu Clubhouse, people were grilling up chicken and barbecue, giving it out for free. . . .

I arrived back at the hotel, soaked and greasy and happy, and walked into my friends' suite, where there was supposed to be some visiting and cocktailing. The couple to be married were there in crisp clothes, being visited by a couple who were childhood friends of the bride, the man in a starched pinpoint Oxford shirt and khaki slacks, the woman, as I remember, in a pink Lacoste shirt and a lime-green skirt, both suntanned and healthy looking. My entrance, like Rod Taylor's staggering into the scientists' meeting with his torn shirt and dirty face after his trip in the Time Machine, was the topic of interest. Where had I been?

I told them all about it—the neighborhoods, the

people catching beads and cups, handing out free beer and food. My friends smiled enthusiastically as they listened to the story, but the other couple listened politely but with puzzled expressions. When I finished the Short Version, they asked, "Weren't you afraid?"

The question surprised me—it had never occurred to me to be afraid—and I remember laughing. "Are you kidding?" I said. "Everyone was in such a good mood." I started repeating it all: the food and drink and the trinkets and souvenirs . . .

"Of course they were in a good mood," the woman said, suddenly. "They were getting something for nothing."

I was so surprised by this remark—I remember almost not believing that I had heard it—that I was literally speechless. I had never heard someone say something like that seriously as an adult. I couldn't locate an appropriate real-time response in my repertoire of possibility, and so I sat there in silence, trying to locate one, and gazing at her.

After maybe seven full, long seconds of tense silence, someone said, "Well. . . . We should probably be heading out. It's so good to see you again. . . ." And that was that. I said nothing to them as they left; it was my first encounter with a phenomenon that I have encountered many times since, in many guises, both crude and sophis-

ticated. Sometimes the sentiments are stated crudely because the speaker can't conceive that I, being white, might
not share his opinion (like the barber who told me as he
was clipping my hair that he didn't gamble on the river-
boats because he didn't like gambling next to niggers);
sometimes they come in the form of subtly coded state-
ments, oblique and ambiguous, put out as feelers to gauge
my reaction.

But that, as they say, is an old, old story. Of course, in
discussing such problems, cause-and-effect relations are
rarely clear-cut. Causes become effects, and vice versa.
*Who started it? Who is to blame?*—these questions can easily
become problems in themselves. But as a general working
principle, isn't it reasonable to expect people with the advantages of good education, financial assets, and opportu-
nities to lead the way in their behavior? Is it fair to say to
those who have no resources to help them, "*You* start. *You*
be noble, you be big-hearted and generous and forgiving,
you have the insight and the wisdom that we always say is
the result of education and enlightenment. Then we'll
talk about it. . . ."? It is one of the ironies that so often
the poorest people do exhibit exactly those behaviors, despite the apparent contradiction. They do it to save themselves; often that humanity is all they have left. To some of

them, certainly, humanity seems a luxury for suckers, just as it does to any number of investment bankers and risk arbitrageurs and real estate developers. It's just that one might reasonably expect more of those who have had the advantages.

# 6.

I never thought that much about Mardi Gras before I lived in New Orleans. I dismissed it, out of ignorance, as another manifestation of the Bourbon Street syndrome—the exaggeration of the obvious, a chance for ordinarily straitlaced folks and fraternity brothers to have some kind of toxic sybaritic freakout before returning to real life. And of course there are dimensions to Mardi Gras that fit that description. But it misses the point, catches only a small part of the surface of the day.

James Gill's book *Lords of Misrule* lays out the history of Mardi Gras, its roots in the nineteenth century, and the purpose it serves for the city's business and social elite. To many New Orleanians, Mardi Gras is not just the day it-self, but the season leading up to it, in which the city's Mardi Gras krewes, which sponsor all the parades and

balls, hold what amount to a series of debutante cotil-
lions, introducing the daughters of the privileged to the
sons of the privileged. In the two weeks before Fat Tuesday these krewes throw their famous parades. Every night,
people from every class and neighborhood make plans to
meet "at Bacchus" or for Endymion (two of the most
popular parades), picking a corner to meet, bringing food
and drinks in coolers, and often ladders with specially
constructed boxes on top in which children sit to catch
the beads and trinkets that spew from the parade floats like
water from the fountain of life itself.

Those are the happiest and most festive weeks of the
year for almost everyone in New Orleans. The entire city,
high and low, gets dragged into things whether it wants to
or not; the weekend before Mardi Gras is full of parties,
out of town visitors and revelry, all culminating in the
Day Itself. What looks on quick examination like a day
when everyone is issued a license for the total stripping
away of inhibitions is in fact something more subtle, in-
volving not a dulled but a heightened awareness of, or
sensitivity to, possibility.

If you have never been to New Orleans on Mardi
Gras, I hope that we will both get that chance again. It is
rare indeed to have every, or almost every, citizen in a city

tuned to the same channel at the same time. Everyone agrees to have a day, the same day, in which no one can be certain what is going to happen. People light out in the morning, often wearing masks or costumes that advance an alternate persona for themselves. They may have certain stops that they know they will want to make, but they are also open to the fact that the winds of the day may lead them elsewhere, and that that is part of the point of it all. One submits to the multifarious flow of chance and felicity, of music and motion.

The best Mardi Gras starts early and ends late. One knows implicitly that all over the city others are doing the same thing, making their preparations to get out into the day, and maybe even encounter you. Maybe the sun is barely up as you roll out of bed and get into your pirate outfit, or your nightrobe and hip waders or your ballet skirt, packing up some water in a pack and head out. One good thing to do if you can manage to be someplace at 7:00 A.M. is to show up in front of Commander's Palace restaurant on Washington Avenue, right across from one of the city's ancient cemeteries, where clarinetist Pete Fountain always assembles the members of his Half-Fast Marching Club to walk along with him and his band as they parade up to St. Charles Avenue and then downtown

toward the French Quarter. Across town Mardi Gras Indians are getting into their new suits, helped by wives and
children and friends, getting ready to meet up with the
other members of their gang and strike out across the city.
The members of the Krewes of Rex and Zulu are getting
themselves dressed and into the floats as their parades
form up.

Out on St. Charles Avenue, hundreds of people
from the neighborhoods on both sides of the avenue have
set up lawn chairs, picnic tables, barbecue pits, couches,
and ladders in the grassy area, the neutral ground as it is
called, along the streetcar tracks, and are sitting around in
their makeshift open-air living rooms, waiting for the Rex
parade to overwhelm them with beads and stuffed animals
and doubloons. You can keep walking down St. Charles
to Jackson Avenue, where by this time the sun has usually
risen, casting shadows behind all the people walking, and
sitting on chairs, the police on horseback. It is good to
take out a little breakfast from the Williams Food Market
right on the corner and eat it sitting on the curb, where
someone will ride up on a bike dressed like the Arch-
bishop of Canterbury and greet you and you will realize
that it is your dentist.

Breakfast finished, you can walk up Jackson Avenue away from St. Charles, along the sidewalk, behind the police barricades, where all the folks are getting set for the Zulu parade, the parade that many New Orleans lovers will not miss at any price, the city's great African American parade where the city's black elite and their invited guests dress up in blackface and Afro wigs and grass skirts and rule the streets. You might run into city council president Oliver Thomas smoking a gigantic plastic cigar and handing out lacy bikini panties emblazoned with the Zulu logo. Or, best of all, you might be graced with a gilded coconut, which the members of Zulu and their families spend weeks decorating—each one is different— with gold paint and sparkles and a dramatically prominent Z. They used to throw the coconuts, but many concussions later they were made to stop; now they lower them to street-level partiers in plastic bags.

Everyone is trying to find a standing place along the barricades, although during the parade proper, people regularly break free and approach the side of the floats to be handed a coconut or other prize, like a special Zulu plastic tambourine. Zulu is a long parade, one of the biggest, boasting an endless stream of marching bands, baton twirlers, drum and bugle ensembles, color guards, as most of the parades have, but they all seem to give it a little something extra for Zulu.

Then the parade comes, like a weather front coming in. It doesn't come all at once; first there are the police cars, with their lights flashing and sirens burping and squawking, pilot birds, disturbed by and warning of the storm to come. Then the breeze picks up slightly as mounted horsemen pass by, scattering doubloons, often with the mayor on horseback, too, accompanied by a police honor guard. Slowly the first floats approach, pulled by tractors, with maidens and various honorees and their attendants throwing beads and waving to their friends in the crowd. Then the Queen and King of Zulu, each on his or her own float, the King sometimes a national luminary with New Orleans connections, more often a local business or civic leader. In 1949 Louis Armstrong himself was King of the Zulus, which he said he considered the highest honor ever bestowed on him. Twenty-three years before, in 1926, he even made a recording with his Hot Five entitled "King of the Zulus," which those not from New Orleans assumed was an African fantasy.

The King and Queen are followed by a procession, seemingly endless, of marching bands, dancers, and the rest, and of course the mammoth floats, each a variation on a theme, on which the masked riders wear matching outfits, but always the blackface and wigs; music is constantly wailing over and under the screams and hollers and laughter of the crowd, which surges forward at times, individuals threading through it, drinking and eating. Some hang back a little on the sidewalk, waiting for the float where their brother is riding, or their boss, or a cousin; maybe they will hold up a sign as they pass ("That's it—float number eight—he's going to be the third one from the front . . .") or maybe they will storm the barricades and push up to the float and be showered with beads and toy spears and stuffed bears and a couple of coconuts and more beads, and then stand waving and smiling, jumping up and down as their Friend In Zulu gets pulled along downstream, waving back to them.

At a certain point, maybe around 10:00 A.M. or so, you have a decision to make, whether to stay for all of Zulu or to peel off and see something else. One of the best decisions you can make is to walk away from St. Charles, further up along Jackson, through the jubilant crowd, maybe stopping occasionally to see if you can catch a few more strings of beads from one of the Zulu floats, up to Dryades Street where you will hang a left and

head uptown a few blocks to the H&R Bar, where you
know some Mardi Gras Indians will be gathering. The
H&R has always been the home base of the Wild Magnolias and their Big Chief, Bo Dollis. It is still the place
where they meet on Mardi Gras morning, even though
the bar had a fire a couple of years ago and is little more
than the original sign and some steps leading up into a
charred interior. New Orleanians are attached to tradition, which is fused to a sense of place, to the ground itself, and that, too, is something to remember in the
aftermath of Hurricane Katrina.

Outside the H&R, and the bar down on the corner
that has taken over the dispensing of libations and conversation from the H&R, you will run into people you
know, black neighborhood folks and white hipsters, par-
taking of all the traditional refreshments and libations of
the season; maybe old John Sinclair will be there with his
King Tut beard and his booming laugh, taking it all in
with his narrowed street-seasoned eyes and his seraphic
smile. The Indians used to come out of the yawning dark
doorway of the H&R one by one, hollering their prowess
to the street, toasted by all; now they gather from the four
corners of the crossroads, often in pickup trucks carrying
their elaborate suits, with Chief Bo as the center, dressed,

in 2005, in bright red feathers, with beadwork that should be in a museum and probably will be someday, whatever is left of it after the flooding.

There is nothing better than standing out there, among friends known and unknown, appreciating the pure thereness and nowness of the moment, which you experienced last year and you hope to experience again next year, a thereness and nowness that hovers above the street level of contingency and passing time, and connects you back to a place that is the ground of being itself. And maybe while you are hovering there, vibrating to that frequency, to which everyone else is tuned, too, you will hear the tambourines and drums from way down the block, the chanted refrains:

> Gonna take my gang on Mardi Gras day
> *Shallow water, yo mama . . .*
> Say mighty coody-fiyo get the hell out the way
> *Shallow water, yo mama . . .*

. . . and if you are really lucky it might be Monk Boudreaux, Big Chief of the Golden Eagles, dressed in glorious purple, come to meet up with Chief Bo and exchange Indian wisdom and fire water and show each other how pretty they are before each one leads his gang off into the still-waiting day.

Eventually, in the afternoon, you will probably end up in the French Quarter, after first paying homage to Rex along St. Charles Avenue. Along Bourbon Street is all the stuff they make the videos out of each year, college girls looking up at guys on balconies who look down and entice them to lift their shirts and give them yet another peek at a Promised Land they will never attain, in exchange for a tossed strand of beads. Down on street level the girls who go in for this are surrounded by boyfriends and classmates and fellow exhibitionists and degenerates-for-a-day and degenerates-for-life, and fringe folks already stewed, smiling like lazy cats with unfocused eyes.

If you keep walking away from Canal Street to the lower Quarter you will eventually come upon gay Mardi Gras. Gay Mardi Gras is probably the apogee of inventiveness for those who like costumes. There are all the obvious culture heroes and touchstones abroad in the streets—many Marilyn Monroes, many nuns, many schoolgirls in short plaid skirts and hairy legs—along with costumes that defy verbal rendering, masterpieces of avant-garde sculpture and cultural discourse, alongside big pink bunny rabbits and old queen couples who have been together for years who decided to go as Laurel and Hardy this year, prodigious dragsters in evening gowns and heavily made-up faces, dripping with pearls and hauteur. On one of the Bourbon Street corners there is usually a stage set up where some demi-monde celebrity is presiding over a costume contest, just shouting distance from alleys that the tourist families, who are mixed in with the rest of the crowd, lead their children past quickly.

Eventually the day winds down. As you make your way back home for whatever post-day meeting you have arranged with friends to recap all the crazy things you saw, or did, or maybe to pointedly not go into it, but at least to make a first tentative step back to normal life over some sacramental food at some traditional location, you might run into the Truck Parade, which follows Rex the way a grotesque satyr play might follow a serious drama. The truck parade—big, noisy, sloppy, raucous—is just what it sounds like. Hundreds of people who lacked the money or the social connections to hook up with one of the mainline krewes hire trucks to tow plain raised trailers that they decorate as well as they can, stocked with recycled beads and trinkets from previous years (instead of buying new stuff at Mardi Gras World, the way the main krewes do), and get hammered as they follow Rex into another year's history, truck horns honking and bellowing and the day's stragglers and diehards jumping up and down and hollering for one more strand of beads, just one more, before all glory passes for another year.

And if you are lucky again, very lucky, you might end up at someplace like Crescent City Steaks, out on Broad Street, an old-fashioned steakhouse with an old-fashioned multi-colored neon sign from the late forties, and old-fashioned enclosed wooden booths where you can draw an ancient curtain for privacy, or sit at a table out on the small-tiled floor under the bright lights, televisions going in the corner and revelers pouring in, some still in costume, and have some drinks and eat a steak and lyonnaise potatoes and be glad, so glad, that your friends are sitting across the table from you one more time. And all across the city, in living rooms and dining rooms and corner bars, in dives and high-class parlors, in dens and on porches and in bedrooms, in the Ninth Ward and the Seventh Ward, Mid-City and Back o'town, Carrolton and the Irish Channel and Broadmoor and the Garden District and Gert Town, the French Quarter and the Bywater and the Faubourg Marigny, everyone is saying the same thing: thank you for this beautiful day, thank you for one more day, thank you for this beautiful food, thank you for this wine cooler that my brother-in-law brought over, thank you for this bed because I can't stand up, thank you for passing the potatoes, thank you for everything, thank you, thank you.

# PART II

# 7.

Two weeks after Hurricane Katrina, I went back to New Orleans for the first time, to see what was left of my place, of my partner Mary's place, of the city.

For two days beforehand my neck was in constant spasm and my viscera turned to water. Muscle aches, fatigue. It wasn't from fear of stray marauders; by mid-September, the city had been placed solidly under the control of the army, the National Guard and U.S. Marshals and God knew who else. I was partly afraid to see what had become of my collections of music and books from the last thirty years, partly afraid to see what had happened to Mary's house, and, more than either of those, I was afraid to see what had happened to the city itself. I felt dread, as if I were about to enter a morgue to view the body of my best friend.

Information had been sketchy about what to expect en route. I would be driving down Interstate 55 for most of the trip, through the heart of the Mississippi Delta, south from Memphis and past Jackson and on into Louisiana. There had been reports of three- to four-hour waits at gas stations throughout that stretch, and I had delayed my trip until I was sure there would be enough gas to get me back.

There was also the question of being able to enter the city. The military had secured all the roads leading in, and everyone needed to show some kind of government, emergency, or press identification to be allowed back. A friend at a magazine had sent a letter saying I was on assignment for them, yet I knew I couldn't hand a National Guardsman a letter at a checkpoint. People who spent their lives honoring the Iron Chain of Command respect hardware, and I needed something laminated. The Louisiana Press Association performed the required alchemy on my letter, turning it into a plastic photo ID with the word PRESS in bright red letters across the top, and a red lanyard from which it would hang suspended around my neck.

I gathered all the information I could about conditions, about areas where there might or might not still be flooding, about the best ways to enter and to navigate certain parts of the city, about military checkpoints en route. There was still no electricity in most of the city. Where there was running water at all, it was not even safe for bathing, let alone cooking or drinking. Even though cleanup operations had been underway for most of a week, there was still debris everywhere, fallen trees, downed wires, nails and roofing materials littering the streets. The uptown neighborhood where I lived had apparently escaped the worst, although Mid-City, where Mary lived, had flooded badly. The last report we had had, from a friend who had been doing animal rescue on a boat, was that the water level had come down several feet from its highest point, and now was level with her porch. That meant that, for at least a week, the first floor of Mary's house had probably been under three feet of flood water, perhaps more.

"Water" was a euphemism. No one knows for sure everything that was in the soup that flooded the city, although what is known—oil, lead, asbestos, human waste, human remains, benzine, battery acid, chemicals from chemical spills—was enough to scare even the military personnel I would encounter so often during my visit.

I bought two pair of cheap rubber boots, which I would use to enter flooded areas and then throw away, and several pair of neoprene gloves. I bought a couple of heavy-duty face masks to filter out not just bad smells but chemical and particle elements, and a jumbo box of heavy-duty garbage bags, and paper towels, and flashlights, and I bought a big orange bucket to carry it all in. I also bought a flat of half-liter bottles of water, and a bunch of plastic boxes and tubs into which I would place all the things that had been most valuable to me and that I planned to rescue. Then I rented the biggest minivan I could find and headed out.

I left on Wednesday, September 14. The drive through the upper reaches of I-55 was uneventful, the sky clear and the air warm. The landscape was familiar to me from drives back and forth to Missouri on holidays in years past, piney woods, rolling hills, occasional clear-cut patches of hillside bordered with a sharp treeline and maybe a long driveway leading across the exposed, treeless land to a bare house in the middle of nowhere. The kind of place you lived, I supposed, if you didn't want to be ambushed.

I stopped in Jackson, about two hours and forty minutes out of New Orleans, filled my gas tank and continued south. Around Brookhaven, Mississippi, forty miles from the Louisiana border, I began to see whole stands of pine trees bent over, mashed down like the bristles of a worn-out toothbrush. In short order I began to see them snapped in half like broken pencils. I spent the night with friends in Hammond, Louisiana, about an hour out from New Orleans; they told me that the wind from Katrina had been so intense that it drove rain through their window moldings. And that was almost a hundred miles west of where the eye had gone through. If the storm had been that bad in Hammond, things were going to be much worse in New Orleans. It took me a long time to get to sleep that night.

The next morning, Thursday, I headed for New Orleans. Just above Laplace, where I-55 fed into east-west running I-10, traffic abruptly began to slow for the first military checkpoint. Traffic was being divided—only emergency vehicles would be allowed to proceed to the left, toward New Orleans on I-10. All others needed to exit right and head for Laplace on route 51, which was a definite ticket to limbo. Almost all the traffic was being directed to the right. As I approached, slowly, I placed myself in the left lane and hoped for the best.

When my car came up to the U.S. marshal who had pulled checkpoint duty, in black T-shirt and fatigue pants, I lifted my laminated ID on its lanyard up so that he could see the bright red word PRESS; he bent down enough to look in, saw it, and waved me through the left side. (The ID turned out to work like a magic spell at every checkpoint. Apparently an earlier order to bar the press from taking photos of dead bodies had created such a backlash that all personnel were now under orders to treat the press like emergency workers.)

I had the interstate almost completely to myself. Through the wild swampy reaches of the Bonnet Carré Spillway, the only other vehicles traveling my way were the very occasional trucks or cars with government or emergency lettering on the side. Along the spillway I saw railroad gangs doing track repair. As I entered Kenner, ten miles out from downtown New Orleans, something seemed odd on a subliminal level. After a moment I realized what it was. I was passing right by Louis Armstrong Airport, and there was no air traffic at all, except for large military helicopters, which were a constant presence, crisscrossing the city all day.

Now I drove along I-10 through Kenner, a stretch I knew very well, and I was shocked by what I saw. At first glance it seemed to be mostly regulation hurricane damage—roofs missing, enormous trees uprooted, boats and cars at odd angles on sidewalks and lawns. But in places I could see evidence of a truly awesome force at work. The entire side of a large storage facility had been stripped away, exposing its innards like a doll house, with people's belongings falling out the side like stuffing out of a couch. As I approached Metairie I saw at least four wrecked billboards twisted at odd angles; their large faces had acted like sails against the wind, which had bent their steel support girders backward like a circus strong man bending an iron bar. Once or twice, the wind had ripped a billboard off its supports and sent it sailing through the side of a building. And this was an area where the residents were being allowed back.

I headed south on Causeway Boulevard toward River Road, which ran alongside the Mississippi River levee, and where there was a checkpoint at the line between Jefferson and Orleans Parishes, the edge of the city proper, the familiarity of the route eerie now, changed as if in a dream. The traffic lights were out, with one or two exceptions, but there was so little traffic that it caused no problems. Every familiar surface had been defaced by the wind and the debris it had hurled in all directions.

On River Road the traffic slowed to a complete standstill. After a minute or two sitting in line I pulled a U-turn and headed up a side road—I knew these roads—

toward Jefferson Highway to see if I could find another
way in. Jefferson Highway was clear sailing for a while,
and I drove through more or less nonstop destruction, past
a small military tent city on the grounds of Ochsner Hospital. At one point, driving along, I saw the Sport Palace, a
dive bar in a low, swimming-pool-blue building, where I
used to play pool when I first arrived in town; it seemed
to be untouched. I slowed down to look as closely as I
could. It *was* okay—Sport Palace was okay! I felt my eyes
well up with tears of gratitude, which was a little silly
since I hadn't set foot in the place for at least ten years. It
was one of my first clues that, while I was managing logistics on the surface, underneath my emotions were going crazy. My shoulders were hunched up and my jaw was
clenched tight.

And then I realized that I was approaching the foot
of the 17th Street canal, the same canal whose own levee
had ruptured near Lake Pontchartrain, flooding Lakeview
and Mid-City. There was a heavily guarded checkpoint,
and as I approached I showed my press badge and was
waved through a rift in a hillock of gravel, where I
swerved to avoid an armada of army trucks heading out
of the parish and found myself heading the wrong way
down Claiborne Avenue. I knew Claiborne Avenue, I

lived not far from here—it was a beautiful place to live, you could get coffee at a little place, they had muffins, too, also juice and teas, and there was the big old-fashioned-looking pumping station and there was no one walking in the empty street and I was in New Orleans again. I was in New Orleans.

Carrolton Avenue, on the way down from Claiborne, was empty. My car followed a path through a snow of saw-dust, wood chips, and shavings—evidence that the big tree chippers had already cleaned up many of the downed trees and limbs. In the neutral ground, empty of streetcars, a city bus sat at a skewed angle, door open, abandoned. There was nobody around at all. At Willow Street a group of five soldiers on patrol with automatic weapons crossed in front of my car. Aside from them, that stretch of street was completely quiet. I felt as if I had entered a house that had been sealed since the occupant's death—things left as they had been.

I turned onto Plum Street, my street, and drove care-fully under several downed power lines; the street itself had been cleared of debris, but there was plenty on the sidewalk and in yards. My house, when I pulled up to it,

had a fluorescent green X spray-painted onto one of the
porch supports—evidence, I guess, that they had checked
for occupants. The area hadn't flooded, so they hadn't
searched inside for bodies.

I got out of the car and the street was quieter than I
had ever heard New Orleans be, even when I had thought
it was quiet. No distant cars or radios. Any sound stood
out in sharp relief, including the periodic deep rattling
ratcheting of helicopters passing overhead. The air didn't
smell bad, not here, but it didn't smell like New Orleans,
either. I climbed the six steps to my porch and took a
deep breath as I put the key in my lock.

Inside my house, things were at least stable. Rain
had gotten in through two large holes in the roof and collapsed the ceiling in two rooms, covering everything with
black silica-like grit and liquefied plaster. It would doubtless take a couple of months to find a roofer who had
time to repair the roof, as well as someone to repair the interior ceiling. Still, I knew this counted as good luck. It
was a mess, but it was a fixable mess. I spent four hours re-
trieving irreplaceable records and books and other personal effects. It was still only mid-September, the heart of
hurricane season, and who knew what might be getting
ready to follow Katrina? There was no air conditioning,

of course, and the temperature was 97 degrees outside, significantly hotter inside. I have never been hotter.

When I got back to my friends' house in Hammond I was so tired I was shaking.

The next day, Mary came down to meet me in Hammond, and we went back into New Orleans together to see about her place, in Mid-City, around where Carrolton Avenue and Canal Streets intersect.

Mid-City is not one of the flamboyant precincts of New Orleans. Its streets are lined with oak trees, and its wood-framed houses are occupied by a mixture of working-class and middle-class families, black and white. It is a real neighborhood; the residents know each other and look out for each other. Once a year, Endymion, one of the largest Mardi Gras parades, passes through the heart of it on the Saturday before Fat Tuesday, and Mid-City is transformed into a vast encampment of celebration, with people carrying couches, easy chairs, propane grills, and all the comforts of home out to the neutral ground on Canal Street, where they often camp out all night to keep the spot from which they will view the parade. The rest of the year the streets are filled with people doing errands, or talking, or waiting for the bus or the new Canal Street streetcar to the French Quarter, or walking over to Mandina's for lunch, or Liuzza's, or Venezia for dinner, or Angelo Brocato's ice cream parlor for dessert.

We knew that Mid-City had flooded. From the same checkpoint where I'd entered the day before, we drove up Carrolton, through empty intersections with dead traffic lights, emptiness in all directions. The farther we got from uptown, the worse shape things seemed to be in. Halfway to Mid-City we began to notice the water lines on the houses, at first only to the steps, or the bottom-most shingle of the structure. We passed the ruins of a huge house that had burned to the ground; all that was left was several chimneys, skinny, tall, and naked.

We couldn't get through the Carrolton underpass at Interstate 10—that underpass always flooded in heavy rain anyway. But now it was two weeks after the heavy rain, and there were generator-driven pumping trucks still there trying to get the water out. From a quick glance, there looked to be about eight feet of water still in the bottom.

We crossed over on Washington Avenue, past Xavier University, and we had the road all to ourselves, steering around occasional downed branches, although it was not a heavily wooded area. We took the overpass at Jefferson Davis Parkway, from which we gazed out our windows in awe. For as far as we could see in all directions there was nothing moving; the city was dead, or at least in a coma.

The other side of the overpass set us down in Mid-City, and it was an altered world. Cars had been abandoned on the high dividing areas in the middle of the boulevard and were covered with brownish-gray silt, as was everything else up to about the six-foot level. The street resembled a dry riverbed, full of unmatched garbage, random artifacts of disruption, single shoes, children's toys. As we passed Tulane Avenue we saw someone's boat smashed through the front windows of a furniture dealer, and, farther down, a car on its roof, upside down like a dead insect.

When we tried to turn onto Banks Street, which was covered with a canopy of oak trees, we could not get through on the proper side; gigantic limbs lay across the two lanes heading away from Jeff Davis, and we drove down the wrong side of the street, no one around to tell us not to. The sidewalks were empty of people, the front steps of houses empty, no one around as we drove, slowly, looking around in disbelief. A week earlier this was a lake. Now each house bore runic signs in orange spray paint, placed there for subsequent searchers, indicating bodies of humans or animals found or not found.

Mary's street was empty, and everything was coated with a layer of light brown dried scum from the receded waters. Before getting out of the van we put on the disposable rubber boots and the neoprene gloves and got our heavy-duty surgical masks ready.

Outside the car the first thing you noticed was the smell. You could manage to walk around and breathe, but the air was fouled. It was sour and unsound, rotting garbage as well as animal decay and stagnant water, something acidic in there too, a chemical aspect. Again, the absolute quiet. The grass at curbside all up and down the block was brown—not brown as dead grass always is, although it was undoubtedly that, but coated with clumped brown sludge. The sidewalk was that same light shade of brown, as was the street, except for the tracks where vehicle tires had worn a path.

Every house on the street was coated with a greasy residue from the flooding, up to a line not quite six feet off the ground. As we opened Mary's low iron gate and walked across the scum-slicked bricks that led to her front steps—the day so quiet—we saw that some of the boards on her porch had buckled; the water line was about waist-high along the front porch-support columns. I realized that I was holding my breath. With my heart pumping hard I turned the key in the front door lock and we entered.

The entry hall was unlit of course, and hot, and it was even darker than it might have been because of the plywood put up on the windows to protect them from wind damage. A window on the right side of the house, which had not been covered, had shattered, littering the floor inside with shards of glass and providing some light. As soon as we took a breath or two of the air inside the house, we wordlessly slipped the surgical masks over our faces.

It was hard to get through the hall; her bookcases themselves had come apart, and her books had spilled and splayed and soaked up water and begun to disintegrate in sad, random piles, all over the carpeting runner, which was unrecognizable. Once a rich red, it was now black, and our feet squeezed water up out of it with every step.

We couldn't get through the hall because it was blocked with waterlogged, ruined books and other debris that had once meant something, so we went to the left, through a passageway in which the wood floors were slick with a black slime, into her small, cozy living room, which was very dark, but not so dark that you couldn't see the thick green mold that had grown all over her couch and her one upholstered chair. On the floor was a gaily painted souvenir of a trip—a little wooden model of a Mexican cart set neatly down by the flood water in the middle of yet another black, soaked carpet. On close inspection, the cobwebby looking stuff that disguised its contours was the same slime that coated the floors. In the next room, small rocking chairs and other chairs that had been set up for evenings when guests would come over to play music were also covered with this stuff that resembled translucent bats' wings, which hung like drapery in folds down to the floor where it continued along, seamlessly. The flood water must have formed a skin on top in the two weeks it had sat there, like a soup under which the fire has died, and as the flooding receded the skin had been left draped over everything below the high water line. This was the same stuff that had dried to a brownish-grey powder outside in the sun on the street and the cars and everything else.

The instruments themselves—guitars, banjos, a fiddle, a dulcimer and a large string bass—were absent. This was a puzzle until we went into the dining room, which is where they had all for some reason floated on the water and eventually came to rest on the floor, their wood warped and distended and ruptured, seams split, all useless.

I would keep describing the scene, but I don't know why. There is no point in describing the kitchen or talking about how hot it was and how wet and unpleasant the surgical masks became, and how when we would pull them off to breathe more easily we would quickly put them back on again despite how wet and nasty they were. Everyone who lives in areas of New Orleans that flooded has his or her own catalog of nightmare images of their familiar and beloved home transformed in this way. Anyone, or almost anyone, from New Orleans certainly does not need to read more.

If you do not live in New Orleans you can try this simple experiment: Put a chalk mark on your wall at a point three feet from the floor, then imagine everything below that line coated with toxic scum, swollen with foul moisture. If this is difficult to imagine, take this book, place it in a sink filled with water and leave it there for a week and a half. Then place the soaked book on the floor and try to imagine the entire floor filled with several layers of such books. If it is still hard to envision this, take all of your books, place them in your bathtub and immerse them in a mixture of water, urine, spoiled food, feces, weed killer from the garage, and perhaps your beloved cat, preferably drowned and bloated. Make sure

to turn all the lights off and to leave the house as nearly
as possible sealed to the fresh air, which, come to think of
it, isn't really fresh air anymore in New Orleans. If this
suggestion seems odd, out of the spirit of this book, as if
the author has suddenly turned into an unpleasant
stranger, that is because the author went crazy at some
point that day, not for very long; maybe it was after we
saw the members of the Oregon National Guard, three
houses away under the hot midday sun in the deserted
street, breathing hard, wiping their faces, one of them
getting his boots hosed down with water as he sat trying
not to vomit, and we learned that they had just pulled the
bodies of a pair of elderly sisters from the basement
apartment where they lived and had been trapped in the
rising flood waters. By the time the sisters had tried to
get out the water was so deep that they couldn't open the
door against it, and their windows had locked burglar
bars on them. Or maybe it was just seeing the streets so
empty and knowing that the same thing we found in
Mary's house we could have found in hundreds of others
just in her neighborhood alone, and then the conversation with the members of the 82nd Airborne, wearing
maroon berets and cruising by in a jeep, making sure that
we had a reason to be in the house that we were taking a

break from examining, some of whom had been in Iraq, shaking their heads when we asked if they had ever seen anything like this. Or maybe it was seeing the cat who always hung around our cat, a pathetic little cat everyone called Gypsy, lying soaked and dead on Canal Street as we made the corner when we were driving around with all the streets to ourselves and Mary saying it wasn't Gypsy and me saying, "No, you're right—it wasn't" and trying with all my might to breathe through my nose and not to cry, and succeeding—I got really good at not crying, except for weird moments when you wouldn't have thought there was anything particular to cry about, like a little later that afternoon, trying to describe a second-line parade to a couple of friendly and sympathetic U.S. Marshals who had also stopped to make sure we had business at the house, one of whom was from Las Vegas and one from I think it was Minnesota, maybe it was North Dakota, I'm sorry I can't remember, I can't remember everything, why don't you go down there yourself if you want to know, maybe it was Wisconsin; they were talking about how spirited the people of New Orleans seemed to be, amazed at the friendliness and combination of fatalism and defiant optimism, and I smiled as I heard them talk about it, and started to tell them about how I felt

about just that same fact when I started weeping uncon-
trollably.

There really is no particular reason to keep describing it; we spent the day there, took what we could, secured
the rest as well as we could, and began the long drive back
to Missouri. And, again, if you are yourself from New Orleans there is no reason at all to keep thinking about any
of this, unless you are like the very privileged uptown
white woman in late middle age whom I talked to just a
few days ago, a property owner who lives in one of the
parts of Uptown that had not flooded and whose property
is just fine and who has had electricity for most of a week,
since she returned from her relatives in Boca Raton, and
who couldn't really see what all the fuss was about—after
all, she had running water, her house had electricity, and
everyone on her block was back having a fine time, the
only problem of course being that it was so hard to find
help—it never used to be, of course—good help, yes, but
there were always many others waiting. The tenants in
one of her many rental properties had not yet gotten in
touch with her, although her phone had been back on for
four days—can you imagine?—and her friend at the state
attorney general's office had told her that she was within
her rights to place their belongings out on the street if she

hadn't heard from them by October 25. "I don't *want* to," she said, drawing out the word *want,* "but there are a lot of people looking for places to live." And anyway the severity of the disaster had been so overstated on the news—all that focus on the Ninth Ward and all that. "The Ninth Ward isn't New Orleans," she said to me. "You can come to New Orleans a hundred times and never even see the Ninth Ward."

So true, I thought—and that kind of savage, self-satisfied, ignorant attitude of large numbers of the criminally oblivious privileged is also a part of New Orleans. God plainly loves them because they have electricity, and it is also plain what God thinks of those who don't. They hold many of the purse strings, and they will be trying with everything they have to determine the future of the city.

As soon as we crossed the parish line heading out of New Orleans I began to feel slightly better. Jefferson Parish was not exactly up and running—still no electricity or various other services—but it was farther along than Orleans Parish. For one thing you would occasionally see another car or even a person walking along the street, although it still felt like a ghost town, full of wreckage and silence. But as we headed along Jefferson Highway toward Causeway, we were shocked to glimpse a group of people sitting outside a low green building with a sign that said DECKBAR COUNTRY STORE. As we passed, one of the guys out there held up what was almost certainly a beer can in salute. People outside, enjoying the afternoon; it felt like a hallucination. Mary and I looked at each other in disbelief. We hit the brakes, and as soon as there was a break in the median we made the U-turn and circled back, pulling into the gravel parking area.

It could have been a regulation Friday afternoon in the Bywater: a dozen citizens sitting at picnic tables, sipping beverages, eating chips, talking and just looking out at the road. There were a mother and her seven-year-old-daughter in a Catholic school uniform, a former high school teacher I had met at a parade years ago, several guys who looked like roofers or house painters, an out-of-work drummer, and a couple of unidentifieds who didn't talk much. There was a pickup truck parked nearby painted purple, green, and gold, the Mardi Gras colors, with beads and other artifacts hanging from mirrors.

Inside the dark, cement-floored store, where the lights were still off, a woman known as Sister was dispensing free sodas and beers and sandwiches. "We got plenty. We never know what we're gonna have, but we'll have something. Have a sandwich. There's beers in the ice chest if you want one . . ." the familiar sound of welcome, the New Orleans sound. We had a beer—Who knew where this stuff had come from? Who cared?—and I ate a couple of pieces of white bread with a slice of ham inside, and we sat outside at one of the picnic tables, talking to various folks who came and went, and as we sat there the worst of what I had been thinking and feeling in Mid-City began to even out a little, the sense of eerie soullessness and devastation began to be balanced out by just so much with the fact of human contact and communion, a restatement of the fact that we are here, that as long as we are here we can at least eat and drink and make some jokes. "No, we ain't trying to make any money off this. This is all free, as long as we can do it. Take whatever you want." Just to sit outside for a while and share the fact of that moment with some other people was enough to relight that pilot light that had blown out for about a half hour in Mid-City. There was that echo from somewhere, of thank you. Thank you for this sandwich and this cold drink, and for the voices of these other people all around. We sat there for the better part of an hour, and, by the time we left, our spiritual gas tank, which had been below empty, had filled just enough to carry us the next leg of the trip, at least. And if that sound and that feeling could be rekindled in the midst of all that chaos, then I knew New Orleans had a chance.

# 8.

I am writing these words in an unused office upstairs at a cotton gin in Malden, Missouri. Just outside the window nearest the desk where I write, I can see the long, low tin-roofed shed that protects the tractors and trucks and the tarpaulins that will sheathe the huge cotton modules when the cotton is picked later in the fall. Across the gravel parking lot is the gin itself, grey tin and steel, with beige ducts that will blow air and carry off the seeds extracted from the cotton to another place where they will be used in their own way. Silos in the distance.

Malden is in the southeast corner of Missouri, called the bootheel, an area that should probably have been part of Arkansas. This is still the South, not yet the Midwest, although that invisible and porous line is crossed not that far north of here. It is farming country, where the rhythms of nature and weather, the times of the year, are set according to the natural calendar of crops and the market cycles arranged around the harvesting and transport of the crops. My better half, Mary, grew up here and knows these people and this land, and this is where we have been able to come for refuge from the devastation, and we will be here for some undetermined amount of time.

Life here was uninterrupted by the storm. The cotton is about three weeks from harvesting; downstairs at the gin office men in flannel shirts and mesh caps come and go, talking about prices and storage logistics. This part of the country is strange to me, although I have spent many short vacations here with Mary; its rhythms are not the rhythms I grew up with in New York, nor are they the ones I have made my own in New Orleans. And yet it is a place where life is going on as normal, and that is a powerful thing.

It is remarkable how quickly the brain and nervous system can make at least superficial accommodations to absolutely indigestible realities. Images that even a couple of weeks ago constituted an overwhelming and shocking and nightmarish unfolding present-tense reality have begun at odd moments to seem more like history than like a living reality. That is because I am separated from it geographically, and I have been busy, trying to sketch in some kind of provisional near-term future. People to call, and emails to answer, people who want to know how I am, or who want me to speak. The kindness and generosity of my friends—even those with whom I haven't communicated in thirty years or more—has been a comfort. So far none of my New Orleans friends has lost his or her life, although at least twenty have lost their homes along with everything they owned.

New Orleans is my home. I don't know when I will live there again, and for the moment I am physically separated, and the living in a different place creates a kind of psychic undertow, like flesh healing from a wound, whether you want it to or not. The contrast between the normal life being lived by everyone around us and our own experience creates a variety of psychic and emotional dissociation that I will be living with and exploring for the rest of my life.

One reached an overload watching the images on television, even as one couldn't turn away for long stretches. The images were a combination of elements that we hadn't seen before—a natural disaster of the proportions that we associated with undeveloped, rural areas, usually in some other country or continent, but this time occurring in a familiar urban landscape, now changed utterly. One cried, one had one's sleep disturbed, one could not believe what one was seeing. The streets where one drove on the way to dinner, or to a funeral, or to a friend's house, submerged in three, or six, or ten feet of water, only the tops of buildings visible, or the tops of doorways, as if in a science fiction movie about the end of the world. Even for people who had never been to New Orleans it was traumatic to watch; for those of us who live there and who face uncertainty, at best, about what if anything is going to be left of our lives, it has been unbearable. And yet . . . we could turn the TV off when we had had too much, when our hearts were going too fast and we needed to maintain our sanity.

But for hundreds of thousands of others, the television could not be turned off. Those images that I can escape by the flick of a TV switch, when I need to insulate myself for a while, or by closing a newspaper, have been a twenty-four-hour-a-day reality, and will go on to be a powerful, searing, scarring wound, for the people who lived through them in the city, as long as they live. Women who were raped in the chaos that the government was so slow to recognize and take steps to stop, people whose lives ended on a sidewalk where their bodies lay uncovered for days rotting in the hot sun, or trapped and drowned by rising flood waters in their own attics, and the people who saw all that, who smelled all that, even as they were sustaining their own traumas, people who walked through the streets crying, holding onto small children, or who swam through oil-slicked, sewage-filled water, unsophisticated people with no one to call and no idea where to go. And the lucky ones who were rescued, brought to the Superdome, where the roof blew off and the toilets overflowed and the food ran out and so did the medicine. Or were set down by the side of an interstate somewhere on the fringes of the city, or at the Convention Center next to rotting corpses, and eventually airlifted or bused out to Red Cross camps in Iowa and Michigan and Missouri and Oklahoma.

The majority of these people are black, and poor. They are the people, and the descendents and families of the people, who gave jazz music to the world, who dance at parades during the New Orleans Jazz and Heritage Festival, who play in the marching bands, and who cook food for the members of the marching bands. They are the people who drive you in from the airport and make you feel at home instantly, the people who wash out your shower and change your sheets at the quaint hotel you stay at, the ones who clear your table and wash the dishes you eat from at the new favorite restaurant that you tell all your friends about when you get back home, and who gather all the garbage outside all the hotels and restaurants and bars that make up New Orleans for the people who visit it.

They are the ones who figure out a way to buy their children food and diapers and some kind of small birthday presents out of incomes smaller than many college kids' allowances. They sometimes spend two hours on three different buses in the morning getting to a minimum wage job, and do the same thing in reverse at night, and figure out a way to buy blood pressure medicine and diabetes medicine and God knows what else out of their tiny, tiny slice of the great American pie. And when a parade passes, whether it is for one of the Social Aid and Pleasure Club anniversaries or for a funeral, they dance behind it, and laugh and take a little drink, because they know better than anyone that life is short and hard and often bitter but it is at least life.

Those are the people who have been uprooted from the only houses, neighborhoods, customs, landscape, and friendships they have ever known, and they will be experiencing the terrible practical deprivation and spiritual pain of the memories they carry, the age-old pain of exile and homelessness. They and the community they embody have given love and beauty to the world, a precious spiritual resilience in the form of music, cuisine, and spirit that is recognized around the world.

And those affected are not just African American—people of all hues were roused from flooded porches, rescued from attics, huddled on sidewalks, cowering in the Superdome. The old-time Italians and Irish and Croatian and Cape Verdean and all the other groups that built New Orleans, wrought its iron balconies, carved stone for its buildings and laid their bricks, surveyed its beautiful and charming streets—not just the people who owned it and enjoyed it, but the people who built it with a grace and soul that can't be measured in dollars and sense or even compensated for by it. They did it the way they did it out of love, and that spirit is what brings people to New Orleans; the food, the architecture, the music, is just the tangible incarnation of that spirit.

That spirit is in terrible jeopardy right now. If it dies, something precious and profound will go out of the world forever. Maybe not entirely; maybe New Orleans people, black and white, will get together in exile every year and commemorate their holidays and their spirit, Mardi Gras and Jazz Fest, red beans on Monday and barbecue and beer at Vaughan's on Friday evening, and keep it alive in exile as the descendents of the Israelites have kept their faith and their covenant alive. That is up to them. But in the near term, the fate of the place, the sacred ground, that gave birth to all that beautiful and deep spirit hangs in the balance.

By now most evacuees have been moved out of the shelters. The ones with family have moved in with relatives; the Red Cross bought them a bus ticket to Georgia, or to Tennessee, or maybe to another part of Missouri or Oklahoma or Arkansas or Mississippi. Some evacuees with drive, or resources, or who understand how to communicate with the various systems set up to help them, have been transferred to apartments that have been made available for them in cities they had never heard of before this catastrophe. Many more at this writing are living in hotels, paid for by the government, and have no idea what the next step is.

Depending on where you live some may well have

landed in your community, alone or in groups or in small family units. These people probably watched flood water rise on their street and up the steps of their homes; maybe they got out beforehand and headed out of the city if they could, or to the Superdome, or the Convention Center, with a suitcase or with just the clothes on their backs, and then were then evacuated again, to Houston's Astrodome, a big step up from the total chaos in New Orleans though it was a giant tent city, a shanty town under an electric sky, in a constant din, where they tried to set up some kind of base amid the endless rows of cots under the lights, and the constant coming and going of restless neighbors and strangers.

Some were then transported even further, to places like Black River Red Cross Camp. Black River Camp is located about fifteen miles south of where we have been staying, slightly north of Kennett, Missouri, close to some-where called Punkin Center, one of many camps set up to shelter and process people displaced by the disaster. To reach it you turn off the state highway onto the county road, then off the county road onto a small crumbly paved road, and then onto a gravel road, and then drive on that gravel through hundreds of acres of cotton fields. At about ten o'clock on the night of September 4, three buses full

of black New Orleanians arrived at Black River. They
had spent four days being turned away from provisional
destinations in Texas and Arkansas, until an alert bus
driver took it on himself to make a phone call, and not
long afterward they were on their way to the camp.

The camp itself, used for other purposes at other
times, consisted of perhaps twenty-five small one-room
cinderblock structures outfitted with bunk beds, a low-
ceilinged cinderblock dining hall, a one-room recreation
hall with a small basketball court, a meeting hall that
served as a church, where visiting clergy from the nearby
community delivered nightly sermons, and an administration building shared by efficient Red Cross workers and
local emergency response personnel, all of whom were
struggling to figure out how to manage what must have
seemed a small tidal wave of arriving humanity.

Displaced people go through extreme mental and
emotional stress, especially if they have been taken out of
one set of understood social conventions and class assumptions and placed in a context completely foreign to those
conventions and assumptions. One can only guess at the
range of thoughts and reactions when the Black River
evacuees woke up to find themselves in the middle of
nowhere, surrounded by cotton fields, being read a list of

camp rules and schedules by well-meaning, nervous white folks in uniforms. Gratitude at being someplace stable and supervised; paranoia about who lives in the surrounding area and whether they wear white hoods at night; anxiety about how to contact distant relatives in distant cities; questions about family members from whom they had been separated; pure confusion and fear at being pulled out of a place where they more or less understood the rules and set down in a place where anything might be true.

It took a couple of days, but Red Cross personnel and evacuees alike began to get the hang of things. The Red Cross is very good at quickly setting up and organizing basic provisional shelter and sustenance, and organizing eventual transportation to more permanent locations. Their most profound insight into the human spirit is that a tightly scripted daily schedule, and clearly articulated rules governing all aspects of life, is the best way to give traumatized people a sense of structure in the midst of chaotic times. The Red Cross, be it said, was invented by the Swiss. Their approach has many strong points, but a sensitivity to nuance and cultural difference is not among them. A handful of advisers with some knowledge of New Orleans, including Mary, managed to make some suggestions that helped. The Red Cross's assumption seemed to be that the evacuees would arrive with books and spend the days tidying their cottages and reading quietly indoors, showing up promptly for meals, everyone recognizing the importance of a smoothly functioning, schedule-driven mechanism. They had kindly, and somewhat pathetically, provided three decks of playing cards for recreation, to be shared among the 165 people. What were the evacuees supposed to do with the time they had on their hands?

New Orleanians like to sit outside on their steps and talk, and at Mary's suggestion lawn chairs were brought in and placed outside the cabins, and they helped immensely. The Jaycees came and cooked barbecue—not exactly New Orleans cuisine, but a nice try and an appreciated gesture. Sony Music and Rounder Records provided CDs of New Orleans music—Irma Thomas and the Dirty Dozen Brass Band and Johnny Adams and Louis Armstrong. And, slowly, arrangements were made for more permanent, if still provisional, living situations for the evacuees. Contacts were made with relatives, bus tickets were purchased. Local charities delivered clothes and people were able to outfit themselves slightly better. Government-funded housing was located in nearby cities and some landed in apartments in towns where they knew nobody and had no sense of how to get around or who to talk to. Some would catch on quickly and make the most of it, others would need help that might or might not be forthcoming.

Black River Camp lasted about two and a half weeks—a balloon that inflated, and then deflated—before everyone was sent on to their next chapter. The same questions were being asked across the nation in Utah and Cape Cod and St. Louis and Kansas, in rural areas and small cities and major urban areas alike. It was a diaspora of historic, even Biblical proportions; New Orleanians seeped into dozens, hundreds, of communities, like rain into the ground, each with his and her own notions about what would come next, since no one knew, or knows, what the fate of New Orleans itself will be.

I spent an afternoon and evening at Black River Camp about four days after the evacuees arrived. It made me happy for the first time in two weeks just to spend time around New Orleans people, to hear the sound, see the walks, the ways of laughing and listening. The evacuees had more or less adapted to the camp's schedule, and the aid workers had adjusted somewhat to the New Orleanians' tempo. The workers were constantly answering questions about the arrival of bus tickets or the conditions at their eventual destinations or countless other details. I would say that everyone was in some degree of shock; most were functioning surprisingly well under the circumstances. Of course, even before the hurricane most of the people there had found some way of adapting to crowded living conditions at home, or scheduling difficulties, and had learned the virtues of patience, if only in the name of controlling their blood pressure and staying out of jail. These disciplines served them well at Black River. People had figured out a way to get as comfortable as they could, more or less, where they were, but everybody wanted to leave.

Some would not go back to New Orleans. "I feel," one woman at Black River told me, "like I been given a new chance on life." She had arrived in dirty rags and had cooked up a striking outfit for herself, out of relief donations, of bright red blouse and, impossibly, a matching hat. She didn't know where she was headed, but she knew it would be better than where she had been. Silas, a guy in his early thirties who wore a white bandanna unfolded over his head, held in place by a blue terrycloth athletic head band, to keep off the gnats and flies and mosquitoes that were a constant bedevilment ("This my sheik look," he explained), had a girlfriend in Georgia who was going to take him in. "She was asking me to come there *before* the storm hit," he said with a sly smile.

But most of the people I talked to knew they were going back to New Orleans. They talked about their streets, and landmarks we all knew, traded information about friends and neighborhood joints and familiar locales, with a kind of defiant sadness and tenderness and humor. "People born in New Orleans always go back," one woman, about fifty years old, told me. Her home was in the hard-hit Bywater neighborhood, and she was sitting with her friend, suitcases packed, waiting for a nine o'clock bus that would deposit them in Houston the next day, where they would be among relatives. Her friend, sitting next to her on the bench waiting for the bus, agreed vigorously. "Yeah, I'm going back. No matter how long it takes."

That was a phrase I heard several times in one night: "No matter how long it takes." In other words, time was not the consideration; the considerations were located in a timeless zone. This timeless zone is a thing New Orleans people carry within them and can't get rid of, even when they might want to. As they passed the days and nights in the haze and dust, fighting off the gnats and the mosqui-

toes and the flies more or less good-naturedly until a place
had been cleared for them in Atlanta or Hot Springs or
Cape Girardeau, trying to make phone calls, listening to a
local preacher in the evenings, sitting in the lawn chairs
talking or just watching others walking back and forth,
even those who would not go back carried a tempo and
an accent and an attitude with them that they would
never lose.

And what about New Orleans? What is the future of the
culture that came from all those neighborhoods with their
own sense of being, formed over decades and decades,
where parents and grandparents and great-grandparents
had lived? Former first lady Barbara Bush, visiting the Astrodome, told a radio interviewer, "So many of the people
in the arena here, you know, were underprivileged anyway, so this is working very well for them." How could
they possibly miss a place where they were, you know, underprivileged?

How could they miss a place where they knew
everyone on the block? Or where they could walk to the
grocery store and buy food and seasonings out of which
they could prepare meals that were unique to that place

and which they had eaten since childhood and which made them happy? How could they miss a place where there was music all the time, and where they could sit out in the evening on their front steps talking to people they had known for years, and joking in a way that everyone understood, or where their son had gotten dressed in his high school band uniform that they had saved hard-earned money to buy, and then went out to play in the band for the Mardi Gras parade? How could they miss the place where their granddaughter took her first steps, or their father had kept his uniform from World War Two in a cardboard suitcase lined with newspaper?

How could you even say such a thing unless you assumed that people who were—*you know*—underprivileged had no past, no sense of life, no memories and no feelings—in short, weren't really people at all, as we know them? That they were incapable of finding dignity and a reason to live even in the teeth of a hostile situation? The "underprivileged" people of New Orleans spun a culture out of their lives—a music, a cuisine, a sense of life—that has been recognized around the world as a transforming spiritual force. Out of those pitifully small incomes and crumbling houses, and hard, long days and nights of work came a staggering Yes, an affirmation of life—their lives,

Life Itself—in defiance of a world that told them in as many ways as it could find that they were, you know, dispensable.

This may seem obvious to you if you are reading this, but it bears saying over and over again: They are not dispensable. Not to New Orleans, not to America. And any scenario of a rebuilt New Orleans that does not embrace the fact of their centrality to New Orleans, that does not find a way to welcome them back and make jobs and a new life for them, will be an obscenity.

Over the months and years to come there will be a lot of wrangling over that future, a lot of jockeying for rebuilding contracts, for housing bids, infrastructure work, every conceivable kind of work. It will be a land grab of a sort not seen perhaps since the nineteenth century, and maybe not even then. As the funds of good will and compassion start to ebb, as they are ebbing already, two basic attitudes will become more pronounced.

One might be called the top-down approach. Treat New Orleans—emptied, as it has been, of people—as a clean slate. Shocking as it is, more than a month after the hurricane hit, New Orleans is still, for all practical purposes, a ghost town. The entire population has left—an unprecedented situation in modern times in any major city anywhere. The disaster, essentially, will be seen as an historic opportunity to recast New Orleans in some other more profitable form, less ramified and complex, more easily manageable. Top-downers will imagine the new New Orleans as a giant theme park—*Jazzworld!* Invite back just enough of the, you know, underprivileged to staff the hotels and do the chambermaid work and garbage pickup, bulldoze everything you can get away with bulldozing, turn some of it into high-priced luxury condos and put up cheap shanty-town housing for the workers in the places still most likely to flood. If you thought the rebuilding contracts for Baghdad were fat, wait until you hear the cash registers ringing for Jazzworld. And now that all the underprivileged have disappeared and been carefully evaluated for reentry, it is even safer than Baghdad. New Orleans will be the new Las Vegas or, more like it, Atlantic City: a big gaudy façade for all the high-rollers, controlled by mobsters and businessmen who live far, far away and destroy everything they touch, a playground decorated and populated with grotesque caricatures of everything that made New Orleans real and beautiful in the first place, and behind the façade the endless tracts of housing where the help lives.

The other scenario starts from the bottom up, with

the recognition that the thing that makes New Orleans attractive to the people who have supported the tourist industry for all these years, not to mention to the people who live there and pay its taxes, is that it is not a theme park. Certain blocks in the French Quarter show the scars of stillborn efforts to move in that direction, but they have never succeeded. The city of New Orleans has always had, and still has, a unique flavor that comes from hundreds of years of slowly mutating culture. If you have read this far there is no need to restate what has already been written about food, and music, and dance and costume and ritual. These elements depend on one another, and if people who have no sense of what it means and how it works, and no desire to find out, are allowed to destroy that cultural ecosystem there may be a brief boom that will line a lot of pockets in and out of New Orleans, but it will be followed by a collapse as the profits are taken and potential visitors realize that New Orleans is not New Orleans anymore.

And beyond that ultimately practical consideration is something deeper: It would be wrong, on a moral and spiritual level. We are all, by now, used to the fact that there will always be a certain percentage of citizens who will try to strip-mine and suck dry everything they can, who reckon everything in dollars and cents and have no compensating sense of grace or meaning in their lives. Everyone knows about Enron, and WorldCom—in a few years if anyone is reading this you may not remember those two, but there will be new ones, don't worry—and if you have paid attention to New Orleans in the past years you know about the city's debacle with the good people of Harrah's casino, and other casinos past, and that list doesn't end either.

The bottom-up approach starts with what has always been, and what must continue to be, a sense of humanity and spirit without which everything is lost. It recognizes one important fact: New Orleans already has—has always had—the basis of a sound economy, although it has rarely played its cards efficiently. That economy depends essentially on two facts: New Orleans is one of the world's major tourist and convention destinations, and the Port of New Orleans is one of the largest and most important in the world. The city does not need to be turned into Las Vegas. All that will do is make a handful of people richer than they already are, and turn the city into a ruin within ten years, fifteen on the outside. New Orleans needs to recognize what its strengths already are, and build on those.

The oil industry needs New Orleans to be an efficiently functioning port. Every import–export business
that has anything at all to do with the Mississippi River
needs New Orleans to be an efficiently functioning port.
Rebuilding and modernizing and recasting the functioning of the Port of New Orleans is something that the
shipping industry, the oil industry, the food and grain and
textile exporters and importers, and the unions associated
with them, can all agree on, and profit from, creating
long-lasting jobs in the process. Anyone who wants to see
New Orleans take an economic leap past what it has been
might want to think about this fact before the Las Vegas
approach.

The people who visit New Orleans from around the
world do not need another Las Vegas or Atlantic City.
That is not why they come. The one downtown casino
has been struggling from the very beginning as it is. If the
casinos along the Mississippi Gulf Coast, in Biloxi and
Gulfport and Bay St. Louis, are rebuilt—and they will
be—people will go *there* to gamble, as they have for years,
not to New Orleans. People come to New Orleans because they have imagination and they enjoy finding inter-
esting corners. They might be New York or Hollywood
people who email each other back and forth about fantas-

tic restaurants they have discovered, or Midwestern conventioneers peeking into strip joints on Bourbon Street, or jazz fans who search out the corner where King Oliver used to play, or tourists who stroll amazed through the Garden District looking at the mansions and then eat a meal at Commander's Palace, taking the street car or a taxi and marveling at the flavor of this place. Destroy the flavor and you will destroy the reason they come.

As this is being written, in early October, New Orleans mayor Ray Nagin has taken the first steps in exactly the wrong direction, announcing that the city would become Las Vegas South, a gambling mecca, with casinos lining Canal Street and money flowing like champagne.

Nagin is a decent man, but he is not a leader, and his moods have bounced all over during the crisis like ball bearings rolling off a table. From his underplayed, tentative hesitation in ordering evacuation, to his disappearance from the city during the crucial days when he might have been able to visit the Superdome and Convention Center and give the people who elected him a little hope and sense of what was happening, to his heartfelt but overdue public anger at the federal government's slow response to the security situation, to his premature inviting of people back into a city with no garbage pickup, spotty electricity, a police department in disarray, no working hospital, and a contaminated water supply, then his rescinding of the invitation, to his laying off of half the city's labor force only days before his manic announcement of his Las Vegas plan, Mayor Nagin has flailed away at the city's problems like a blindfolded kid waving a stick at a piñata.

New Orleans desperately needs imagination and vision right now, and leaders who can see past their own short-sighted interests. We need to think beyond the unimaginative functionaries and the small-time, charming rogues, and the soulless greedheads who manipulate them. We have to think a little harder about what we are doing as a culture. We have to think a little harder about what is important and what lasts.

At one point, early on, some public figures even asked whether it "made sense" to rebuild New Orleans. Would you let your own mother die because it didn't make financial sense to spend the money to treat her, or because you were too busy to spend the time to heal her sick spirit? Among people who are able to think only in terms of dollars and cents, for whom everything is reckoned in terms of winner and loser, profit or more profit, of course it doesn't "make sense" to rebuild, or to rebuild properly. A lot of things don't make sense in those terms, including every one of the virtues espoused by a Jesus who has helped them win votes but whom they would not invite to their house for dinner if they met him tomorrow, unless maybe he could be useful for fundraising.

Dollars and cents are important. And most of the large-scale good done in the world is done by people who have both money and vision. There are people of immense compassion and good will and love and insight and vision all across the socio-economic spectrum—black and white, poor and rich. The question is not racial solidarity or class solidarity but a distinction between people who have a soul left and people who have mortgaged their souls for a short-sighted self-gratification—whether they are the predatory thugs who roamed the streets of New Orleans after the hurricane raping defenseless women, or the wealthy fat cats who can't see past the next golf green unless there's a stack of money there.

Nobel prize–winning novelist William Faulkner, a one-time New Orleans denizen, remarked during the era of school desegregation that if we were descending to the level at which little girls were being spit on by mobs on their way to school just for the color of their skin, then

maybe we didn't deserve to survive as a civilization. Strong
words, but they echo in my mind now with the strength
of a giant bell tolling. Greed, brutality, short-sightedness,
racism, thuggishness are an abiding part of human affairs;
they will never be eradicated. But we as a country, as a
culture, can decide what we think of them, and what we
want to do or not do about them.

During that first week, a reporter for the *Washington
Post* tracked me down and asked me about the musical
heritage of the city, and if I thought New Orleans could
survive this disaster. Such a natural question, and so impossible to answer. What I said was that if any city could
survive something this deeply traumatic, New Orleans
could. But it will depend on the world giving back some
of the love and human beauty that New Orleans has
given to the world for so long.

The top-down approach is relatively straightforward
and quick and it will ruin something that can never be replaced. The bottom-up approach will take more thought
and maybe more time but it will build a New Orleans that
feels like New Orleans, and that can last. Put in the leg-
work to bring in investment to rebuild what is already
there—the aquarium and City Park, the stores and restaurants and universities and neighborhoods that have been

damaged, the hotels that have contributed to the city's economy for years. There will be plenty of money to go around. Use a Habitat for Humanity model to construct durable and livable and affordable housing for the people who want to come back to the city they love and will work for. Give people a sense that they have a stake in re-building their own lives, a collective project that can make everyone feel proud instead of cheap. That will be in the spirit of New Orleans, and it will pay dividends for the entire country. It is still not too late.

And then maybe next year, or the year after that, we will pass one another on Mardi Gras Day with the sound of a parade in the distance, or a gang of Indians coming down the street, and we can stop and share a drink and a laugh under the oak tree and give thanks once again for this beautiful day, this life, this beautiful city, New Orleans.

# ACKNOWLEDGMENTS

This tragedy touched people across the nation and the world; in the course of it I heard from people I had not seen or talked to, in more than a few cases, for more than thirty years. There is no room to list them all, but their support has made it possible to get through a dark time with an eye on the light.

In Malden, Missouri, where we have made a temporary home, people could not have been nicer. Special thanks must go to Jean Howell, whose patience, kindness, and generosity have been amazing, and to John Howell, Ann Bostic, Clara and Sali Ware, and especially to David Mayberry and the gang at the Stokes-Mayberry Gin, who set me up with a place to work on this book. And to the trustees of Sweetwater Farm, and to Roscoe, who had just a little while to stay here and made the most of it.

Thanks to my friends old and new who went out of their way to arrange readings and speaking engagements for me across the country in the wake of this disaster. I don't know what I would have done without Robert Olen Butler, Elizabeth Dewberry, Joanna Scott, David Gates, Robert Polito, Stephen O'Connor, Ben Marcus, Alan Ziegler, Tim Parrish, Penelope Pelizzon, Tom Hazuka, Rob Cohen, Cate Marvin, Ann Townsend, John Gregory Brown, Martin Jones, Pat Morehead, and Susan Swartwout.

For kindnesses that I will never forget, thanks to Deborah Triestmann, Tim and Winborne Gautreaux, Collie and Connie Nelson, Roy Blount Jr., Susan Hartung, Mark, Cindy, and Erika Woessner, Lolis Elie, Dave Rodriguez, Suzi Stone, Dave Eggers, Rosemary James and Joe De-Salvo, John Hasse, Marc Smirnoff, Jeff Rosen and everyone at Special Rider Music, Steve Berkowitz and Gretchen Brennison of Sony/BMG, Lauren Calista of Rounder Records, Mike Perry, Eric Banks, the Louisiana Press Association, Elaina Richardson and Candace Wait of Yaddo, Sheila Pleasants of the Virginia Center for the Creative Arts, Warren Zanes and John Goehrke of the Rock and Roll Hall of Fame, Leslie Gerber, James Marcus, Alex Balk, and my mom, Lillian Piazza, whose wisdom and goodness have always helped me find my way.

My editor at ReganBooks, Cal Morgan, urged me to write this book, then provided the soundtrack and brought it all in for a landing; thanks won't suffice but I guess they'll have to do. The same goes for everyone else at ReganBooks, especially Judith Regan, Cassie Jones, Vivian Gomez, Timothy O'Donnell, Lawrence Pekarek, Paul Crichton, and Elizabeth Yarborough. Thanks, too, to Amy Williams, my invaluable agent and friend.

And, above all, thanks to Mary Howell, for much more than I could ever put into words. Are you going to eat that olive?